Matthew M. Vriends, PhD

The New Bird Handbook

Everything about Housing, Care,
Nutrition, Breeding, and Diseases

With a Special Chapter on Breeding Pet Birds

Color Photographs by Paul Kwast and the Author

and Drawings by Michele Earle-Bridges

BARRON'S

The color photos on the covers show
Front cover: Red Avadavat (*Amandava amandava*) (India, Pakistan, Nepal, SE. Asia); inside front cover: Imperial parrot (*Amazona imperialis*) (Dominica); inside back cover: Gouldian finch (*Chloebia gouldia*) (N. Australia); back cover: top left, clockwise: Peach-faced lovebird (*Agapornis roseicollis*) (Africa); Parakeets (*Melopsittacus undulatus*) (Australia); Lesser sulphur crested cockatoo (*Cacatua sulphurea*) (Indonesia); Dama thrush (*Turdus citrinus*) (Asia); Zebra finch (*Poephila guttata)* (Australia) and Scarlet macaw (*Ara macao*) (South America).

All inquiries should be addressed to:
Barron's Educational Series, Inc.
250 Wireless Boulevard
Hauppauge, NY 11788

International Standard Book No. 0-8120-4157-7

Library of Congress Catalog Card No. 88-34973

Library of Congress Cataloging-in-Publication Data
Vriends, Matthew M., 1937-
    The new bird handbook.

    Includes index.
    1. Cage birds. I. Title.
SF461.V734   1989   636.6'86   88-34973
ISBN 0-8120-4157-7

Printed in Hong Kong

20 19 18 17 16 15 14 13 12 11

About the author:
    Matthew M. Vriends is a Dutch-born biologist/ornithologist who holds a collection of advanced degrees, including a PhD in zoology. Dr. Vriends has written more than 80 books in three languages on birds and other animals; his detailed works on parrotlike birds and finches are well known. Dr. Vriends has traveled extensively in South America, the United States, Africa, Australia, and Europe to observe and study birds in their natural environment and is widely regarded as an expert in tropical ornithology and aviculture. A source of particular pride are the many first-breeding results he has achieved in his large aviaries, which house more than 50 tropical bird species. Dr. Vriends and his family live near Cincinnati, Ohio. He is the author of two of Barron's Pet Owner's Manuals, *Lovebirds* and *Pigeons*.

Photo credits:
    Paul Kwast: front cover; pages 19 top, 29 bottom, 50, 67, 68, 77, 78 top, 112, inside back cover, back cover (dama thrush, zebra finch); Matthew M. Vriends: inside front cover, pages 19 bottom, 20, 29 top, 30, 39, 40, 49, 78 bottom, back cover (scarlet macaw, lesser sulphur crested cockatoo, red-faced lovebirds, budgerigars)

Addtional photos:
    P. Leysen: page 111; Fons Mertens: pages 9, 10

Important note:
    The subject of this book is how to take care of various pet birds in captivity. In dealing with these birds, always remember that newly purchased birds—even when they appear perfectly healthy—may well be carriers of salmonellae. This is why it is highly advisable to have sample droppings analyzed and to observe strict hygienic rules. Other infectious diseases that can endanger humans, such as ornithosis and tuberculosis, are rare in many pet birds. Still, if you see a doctor because you or a member of your household has symptoms of a cold or of the flu, mention that you keep birds. No one who is allergic to feathers or feather dust should keep birds. If you have any doubts, consult your physician before you buy a bird.
    Most food insects are pests that can infest stored food and create a serious nuisance in our households. If you decide to grow any of these insects, be extremely careful to prevent them from escaping from their containers.

Contents

Contents

Foreword

This treatise on the care and management of pet birds is a magnificent gem of information which has long been needed.

Dr. Vriends has done a masterful job of combining "know-how" with "care-how." Pet birds are, after all is said and done, not merely ornamental or amusing objects to be kept as toys—they are indeed living sentient beings with needs and interests of their own. Dr. Vriends has managed not only to point out to us those needs and interests, but he has also supplied us with the information which will enable us, as responsible bird caretakers, to meet those needs and interests in an intelligent, caring, and meaningful fashion. Our lives—both avian and human—will be far richer for this knowledge.

Alice DeGroot, MS DVM
March, 1989

Preface

In our country there are some tens of thousands of bird fanciers who gain tremendous pleasure from the care and breeding of birds in cages and aviaries.

Who can fail to delight in the splendor of color, the variety of form, and, above all, the musical ability exhibited by our feathered friends? It is no surprise that there are so many enthusiasts who like nothing better than to surround themselves with birds, perhaps in the house, on the porch, or in the garden, giving themselves the opportunity of admiring the magnificent colors or enjoying the jubilant song at any time.

Have you ever heard the clear notes of the Pekin robin or the sparkling song of the green singing finch? Have you ever admired the amazing colors of the orange weaver or the Gouldian finch? Have you ever seen a hen Chinese painted quail accompanied by a brood of little chicks, each no bigger than a sturdy bumblebee?

This book is designed to give practical advice on the care of cage and aviary birds, hopefully leading the fancier to many years of maximum enjoyment from his or her chosen hobby. It does not pretend to be a scientifically oriented treatise on ornithology or zoology, but is written in a style that can be understood by even beginning fanciers. The book is based not only on the author's many years of experience, but draws freely upon the combined knowledge of generations of expert aviculturists.

The author understands that beginners might be apprehensive as they discover the types of diseases that birds can come down with, the daily food required, and the various pitfalls that can lie in the path of successful aviculture. However, do not let this put you off. Normally birds are healthy, fit, and full of the joys of life. But this does not mean that bird keeping is not a serious responsibility. It must always be remembered that captive birds are fully dependent on the fancier for food, accommodation, and care. Without your care and devotion *they will not make it!* Keeping birds is a hobby that can be indulged in on as limited or large a scale as the individual wishes. The pleasure that comes from success with birds is the same with one pair as with many; and if they remain colorful, sing heartily, stay healthy, and especially breed regularly and successfully, you have the best proof that everything is to their liking. Such success will give you great personal satisfaction. Breeding birds presents the challenge of successfully propagating a species and offers the gratification that comes from working closely with the beauty of nature.

This book would not have been produced without the help and goodwill of many ornithologist friends and fellow aviculturists. I especially thank my wife, Mrs. Lucia Vriends-Parent, for her support and her invaluable assistance during the preparation of the text; to my two good friends, the avian veterinarians Alice DeGroot, MS, DVM, and Stephen Wehrmann, DVM, for their critical reading and appraisal of the final text, and to Mr. John Coborn of Australia for his editorial guidance and his ready help in all matters relating to this book.

All the opinions and conclusions expressed in the following pages are my own, however, and any errors must be my own responsibility.

Matthew M. Vriends
Loveland, Ohio
Spring, 1989

For my daughter, Tanya, with love—
"Soyons fidèles à nos faiblesses."

Considerations Before You Buy

Choice of Species

This may seem an easy task, but when you are standing in a shop surrounded by birds galore, it suddenly becomes a daunting problem. Fanciers are frequently overwhelmed by the array of splendid specimens—one apparently prettier (and perhaps more expensive) than the next. The temptation to buy all, or most, of that beauty can be very strong. I can say with certainty, however, that if you set about acquiring birds with such an attitude you are courting disaster. The end result could be that your initial enthusiasm will be dulled or even lost forever. When birds are purchased solely for their attractiveness, without sensible planning, you take the risk of bringing together specimens that cannot tolerate each other. Fighting soon develops and the astonished newcomer to the field may be witness to a bloodbath. Careful consideration is therefore essential before even a single bird is purchased.

Keeping birds is a fantastic hobby and a leisure-time occupation second to none. The serious fancier who goes about this hobby in a conscientious manner will enjoy a bit of nature at home. Years of pleasure can be derived from a cageful or aviary of colorful feathered friends. Even daily cares and problems will be forgotten while you pursue this hobby. There are a great many bird species, each with a different character. There are birds that can be kept singly in a cage; there are also those that can be kept in the community aviary. There are singing birds, colorful birds, big birds and little birds, ground birds, tree birds, parrotlike birds, little doves and many more. You must decide in which direction you intend to go.

What Kind of Bird Is the Right One for You?

What do you require—a single bird in a cage, or a group of small birds in an indoor aviary? Do you want a garden aviary and, if so, will you need planning permission from the local authorities? If you live in rented accommodations, will the landlord approve? Do you want to breed birds? Do you feel more attracted to the song or the colors of birds? These are just a few of the possibilities and initial problems, which we will now examine in greater detail.

The most popular form of bird keeping has always been the single bird in a cage. In such cases, the purchaser's motivation is usually the bird's song and its companionship rather than the attractiveness of its plumage. One does not need to look far to find many fanciers who own a tame parrot, or a singing cock canary. The canary is the oldest songbird we know, but it must be admitted that "his song makes him." There are many kinds of canaries! Those that come immediately to mind include rollers, waterslagers (trillers), American singers (a cross between the roller and the border fancy), and

Choice of species. Careful consideration is essential before even a single bird is purchased. Top left: silverbeak (seedeater); top right: diamond dove (seedeater). Center: Pekin robin (soft–bill). Bottom left: macaw (seedeater); bottom right: turquoise parrot (seedeater).

7

Considerations Before You Buy

Harz canaries. The Harz canary has a very melodious and deep song, which the experts regard highly. One drawback, if one can call it a drawback, is that the Harz canary's plumage is not the most beautiful; it is usually green or green-yellow pied, but wholly yellow specimens are sometimes available.

Should you prefer a canary with more colorful plumage, there are many possibilities among the color varieties. These include dilute greens (agate), cinnamons, reds, white ground, opal slate, etc. All of these colors are currently very popular and thus easy to obtain. Note, however, that although these birds have particularly attractive plumage, their song is often loud and harsh, though not particularly unpleasant.

The waterslagers are usually yellow in color. The song is rather harsher than that of the Harz canary, but the waterslager has a greater range of notes. The whole song has a metallic or watery tone.

There are, of course, several other bird species that can be kept for their singing ability—some of which make no greater demands than canaries and can be just as inexpensive. One songbird that is well worth considering is the gray singing finch (*Serinus leucopygia*). Like the canary, it is a seedeater and has a particularly dainty and variable song. Its color is mainly grayish, but it quickly becomes tame and very affectionate. You might also consider the green singing finch (*Serinus mozambicus*), which is also known as the yellow-eyed canary. This species has attractive plumage and is relatively inexpensive; moreover, it is also a seedeater and easy to care for. Both of these tropical birds are happy in a sturdy canary cage.

Birds that are somewhat more expensive but well worth considering for their attractive plumage are the Pekin robin (*Leiothrix lutea*), which is also known as the Japanese or Chinese nightingale, and the indigo bunting (*Passerina cyanea*). Both have a very beautiful song and will do well in an indoor cage. The feeding of these birds is somewhat more complicated than that of the seedeaters and they require a special menu that includes mealworms.

Other fascinating species, perhaps more expensive but well worth it, include the tropical starlings and thrushes, for example the shama (*Copsychus malabaricus*), the orange-headed ground thrush (*Zoothera citrina*) and the magpie robin (*Copsychus saularis*). Also consider the golden-fronted leaf bird (*Chloropsis aurifrons*), the silver-eared mesia (*Leiothrix argentauris*), and various South American cardinals.

Should you not want to keep only songbirds, carefully consider your objectives. Do you want to breed birds and observe the exciting natural progression of egg brooding, hatching, and rearing of the young? Or will you be content with a collection of birds chosen solely for the beauty of their plumage and song? In either case there are possibilities for every fancier, whether you are the owner of an outdoor (garden) aviary or a large indoor cage.

For indoor aviaries, society finches (or Bengalese), together with orange-cheeked waxbills (*Estrilda melpoda*), violet-eared waxbills (*Granatina granatina*), and/or red-cheeked cordon bleus (*Uraeginthus bengalus*), etc., are ideal. There are also many possibilities among the more expensive species: for example, the long-tailed finches (*Poephila acuticauda*), Gouldian finches (*Chloebia gouldia*), red-faced parrot finches (*Erythrura psittacea*), etc. Indoor aviaries, each with a single pair of African or Australian birds, are particularly attractive.

If you like to keep soft-billed birds, remember that successful breeding is more likely if you keep single pairs—only in large outdoor aviaries is it worth risking greater numbers together. Should you wish to enlarge your collection at any time, be sure

Above left: The Border canary or "wee gem" best represents what people think a canary should look like.
Above right: The Gibber canary, a breed in which posture and frilled plumage have been combined.
Blow left: The Norwich canary is by far the most famous of all British canary breeds.
Below right: The Scotch fancy was extremely popular during Victorian times..

Considerations Before You Buy

For good breeding results you must ensure that you do not have too many birds in one and the same housing and that the species you have will tolerate each other.
Here, a Green finch cock inspects the nest of a pair of zebra finches. Green finches are known for pulling nests to pieces and making a nuisance of themselves in a community aviary with small finches and canaries.

to obtain specimens that require similar care as the existing stock and ensure that any new bird you wish to buy will fit into the community.

There is one group of birds which we have not yet discussed: the ever-popular parakeets. Many parrotlike species are best kept in outdoor aviaries, but in most cases should not be kept with smaller birds, which would soon be mutilated. The best policy is not to mix parakeets with other species, otherwise disappointments nearly always ensue. Most of the parakeets should be kept as single

Above left: In the Gloucester fancy the crested canaries are known as coronas, the plainheads as consorts.
Above right: The Lizard, known since 1762, was introduced into Britain by the Huguenots.
Below left: The Southern Dutch frill occured first in 1800 in the Netherlands.
Below right: The Belgian canary is also known as the Belgian bult or "Belgian humpback."

breeding pairs in large aviaries, especially if successful reproduction is contemplated. Budgerigars (or parakeets) and lovebirds may be kept in groups in an aviary, but the latter, with the exception of the peach-faced lovebird (*Agapornis roseicollis*), require regular supervision, unless kept in single pairs. Canaries are not usually kept together with other species, but this is due to the speciality of the fancy. Those who wish to breed first-class examples of color or song canaries would rarely have sufficient time or space to keep other birds.

Do You Plan to Breed Birds?

If you plan to breed birds you must be prepared for some disappointments. Birds are not simply breeding machines! With the many different species there are great possibilities for everyone to make a satisfactory choice—even on a small budget. The beginner should first gain experience with less-expensive, more easily kept species which are not too demanding in their care. This is not to say that the cheapest birds are the easiest to breed—nor that more expensive birds are excessively difficult. There have been cases where society finches (Bengalese) have been very bad breeders, and species such as the expensive golden-fronted leafbird (*Chloropsis aurifrons*) have successfully produced one brood after another. With all birds there is one important thing to be borne in mind: They should not be bred too young.

What do we mean by "too young"? Well, the answer to that question is very relative, but in general, it can be said that breeding success is more likely with birds not less than 15 months old—but preferably at least two years old. If you purchase birds of unknown age and they fail to breed successfully, it is more likely that they are too young, rather than "the weather being unsatisfactory."

Or course, it is essential that the birds receive all that is necessary to keep them in the best of health. Never think "They are only birds, why should I give

Considerations Before You Buy

CHOOSING A PSITTACINE

Bird Species	Advantages	Disadvantages
African Gray Parrots (*Psittacus erithacus*)	Good talker and great mimic; however not noisy. Longevity. Intelligent. Reproduce quite commonly.	Unreliable temperament. Often notorious feather-plucker when neglected. Usually a one-person bird.
Amazon Parrots (*Amazona* species)	Excellent cage and aviary birds. Many species have great personalities and are good mimics and talkers. Longevity. Intelligent.	Hard to acclimate. Sometimes one-person birds may become neurotic screechers when confined to small cages. Difficult to breed.
Cockatoos (*Cacatua* species)	Affectionate, especially when hand raised. Longevity. Highly intelligent.	Many species are very noisy and therefore not suitable as house pets. Often notorious feather-pluckers when neglected. Often one-person birds. Very destructive. Many species (especially the Lesser Sulphur Crested) may suffer from psittacine feather and beak disease (PFBD), a stubborn virus infection.
Macaws (*Ara* species)	Affectionate and playful. Longevity. Very intelligent.	Noisy and very destructive. Often feather-pluckers. Difficult to breed. Require large cages which are expensive.
African Parrots (of the genus *Poicephalus;* e.g., Senegal Parrot)	Affectionate. Average mimic and talker. Commonly available. Get along well with other parrots in large aviaries.	Destructive. Caged birds often become lethargic; they prefer a good size aviary. Difficult to acclimate.
Lovebirds (*Agapornis* species)	Hand-reared birds are very affectionate. The peach-faced lovebird (*A. roseicollis*) is the most prolific breeder; many color mutations.	Many species (among them the peach-faced) are impossible to sex on the basis of outward appearance.
Australian Parakeets (*Neophemas,* Rosellas, *Pseptotus,* etc.)	Adapt well to captivity. Long breeding life; highly prolific. *Neophema* species can be kept in a community aviary with parakeet species and finches.	Many larger species are aggressive. Not suitable as household pets, except hand-reared birds.
South American Parakeets (Conures, Aratingas etc.) **and Asiatic Parakeets**	Beautiful colors and nice characters. Very intelligent and inquisitive. Many are prolific breeders. Hand-reared birds make very delightful pets.	Very noisy. Often destructive. Not suitable as cage birds.
Lories and Lorikeets	Colorful. Intelligent. Affectionate.	Difficult to keep, as all (except the Musschenbroek lorikeet) need a nectar mixture, fruits, honey, etc. Susceptible to the fungus *Candida albicaris.*
Cockatiels (*Nymphicus hollandicus*) **and Budgerigars** (Parakeet) (*Melopsittacus undulatus*)	Excellent cage and aviary birds. Prolific breeders with many color mutations; easy to tame. Will learn to repeat a few words when obtained young. Intelligent. Affectionate.	Sometimes noisy.

them expensive food to eat, when they can make do with cheap, inferior food?" This would be a very serious mistake.

A Question of Space

How much space you can spare for your birds is an important question that must be carefully considered *before* you undertake your new hobby. The amount of space will, of course, dictate what kind of birds you can keep. Whether you can accommodate a small show case somewhere in a corner, or whether you can build a substantial indoor or outdoor aviary will determine the choice of numbers and species. Many hobbyists like to use a corner of the attic or garage to build an aviary or set up a collection of cages. If you want to build an outdoor aviary in the yard or garden, the plan should first be discussed with your landlord, spouse, or anyone else who might be concerned. It is better to agree at the outset, rather than have an argument once the aviary is in position. You must also be sure not to take up the whole yard, thus denying others any use of it. An aviary should be a complementary part of a tastefully laid out garden and a pleasure to own.

The next question is, "How many birds can I keep in my aviary?" A simple answer to this is dangerous—it does not depend solely on the dimensions of the aviary. The most important factor in reckoning the number of birds to be kept is the ground area, but you must also consider the type of birds you intend to keep and their individual space requirements, bearing in mind that an aviary with aggressive soft-billed birds is "full" more quickly than one containing a collection of docile little exotic seedeaters. It is advisable to ask yourself another question: "Why do I want to keep birds? Is it to cram as many as possible into my cage or aviary?" Do not overestimate your possibilities. Overcrowding could be lethal for your birds.

A Question of Free Time

With a free Saturday, many people think that they have plenty of free time on their hands. However, this is not the case. Don't think that once a week is adequate for the care of your birds. You must have the time each day to provide fresh drinking and bathing water, and to collect green food and supply insects—tasks which can't be left just for Saturdays. They must be done daily, or at the very least, every second day. Therefore, before you acquire any birds, you must consider how much time *each day* you are going to be able to devote to your charges. Moreover, it is important to observe your birds each day, so that you can quickly spot any signs of sickness (see page 59) or nip any potentially dangerous quarrels in the bud.

Of course, Saturday (or any other free day) can be set aside each week for major cleaning activities. Don't overdo it, however. If you seem to be "living in the aviary," your family may get the impression that the birds are more important than the household! You must develop a routine. If you can spare an hour or so each day and a little longer on the weekends without imposing on your family life, then you will gain much pleasure from your chosen pastime. Never regard the task of looking after birds as a chore; it is preferable to keep fewer birds and enjoy the experience all the more.

A Question of Money

The financial aspects of bird keeping are important, but cost should not deter anyone from taking up the hobby. You do not need to acquire expensive stock. If you have modest means, you can still purchase birds that are just as interesting as the more expensive exotic varieties. You can start with zebra finches, society finches, silver bills, white-rumped finches, budgerigars (parakeets), or lovebirds. Once these have been bred, you can sell the youngsters and use the money to buy more expensive birds, should you so wish. I know a young hobbyist who, on his twelfth birthday, received a pair of zebra finches. Now, at 25, he is the proud owner of an aviary containing very expensive birds, including some that are worth in excess of $1,000. His success was not accomplished from his allowance, but from the money he raised from breeding his birds—and from which he was also able to pay for bird food and maintenance costs!

To gain real pleasure from bird keeping, *always* purchase quality birds from reputable pet stores or breeders and never be tempted to buy inferior stock. Remember, too, that birds are *living creatures*; therefore, you must be sure that what you purchase is healthy. If you buy from a reputable dealer, you will be in a position to ascertain this. Many potential fanciers have given up on the hobby because of early experiences with birds that have died.

How do we know if a bird is healthy? Refer to the chapter Pet-Bird Diseases, Accidents and Injuries (see page 58).

A Question of Longevity

With sufficient care and management, captive birds can reach a ripe old age, perhaps even older than they would in the wild. This is a fact that you really must consider before taking up the hobby. Different bird species live to different ages—some may live longer than humans! Here are a few examples:

Finches (small)	2–8 years
Finches (large)	8–12 years
Canaries	8–15 years
Budgerigars (parakeets)	8–12 years
Lovebirds	10–15 years
Cockatiels	10–25 years
Mynahs	15–25 years
African gray parrots	40–60 years

Amazons	40–70 years
Cockatoos	30–40 years
Macaws	40–60 years
Lories and lorikeets	10–15 years
Conures	10–15 years
Parakeets (Rosellas, etc.)	10–15 years

These figures are, of course, averages; there have been well-documented cases of large parrots, such as African grays and cockatoos, that lived 70 to 100 years and more. I know of budgerigars that lived 22 years, and of a cockatiel that is approaching its thirtieth birthday; a commitment for many, many years!

Acquiring Pet Birds

There are three principal sources of cage and aviary birds: dealers, direct importing, and breeding. Although the cost of quarantining imported

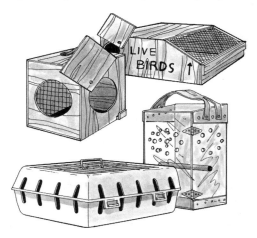

Various bird carriers are available: Top right: A traveling crate must meet airline regulations for size. Cover the whole inside with indoor/outdoor carpeting for padding and warmth. A proper perch must also be included.

birds does affect a bird's retail price, the process can save money in the long run by preventing losses resulting from the rampant spread of disease.

In the United States, a government decree mandates that all birds entering the country be quarantined at least 30 days. This precaution is taken to prevent the domestic occurrence of Newcastle disease, the dreaded viral infection that cost the poultry industry several million dollars some years ago. Imported birds are released into the domestic trade only after they have been medically examined and found to be free of infection.

When birds die during the quarantine period, they are carefully examined and the cause of death is precisely determined. Although expensive, the quarantine system works satisfactorily—even though some groups voice opposition to it from time to time.

Some bird fanciers consider using government-operated quarantine stations to import their own birds. This is no simple matter, however.

First, such a fancier must know reliable sources overseas, and must be prepared for a lot of paperwork. Second, this approach is far from inexpensive: Expect to pay a customs broker between $500 and $1,000 for handling a shipment of birds. Add to this the maintenance cost for each bird, which runs about 30 cents per day. Because the minimum quarantine period is 30 days, this type of arrangement would cost at least $9 per bird for maintenance alone! To that, add the purchase cost and additional charges for transportation to and from the quarantine station. All told, a pair of exotic finches, for example, will cost a fancier $40 or more.

Also, if a bird dies in quarantine, the quarantine station operators are not responsible. You not only lose the bird but also all of the money already spent on it. All in all, it is generally safer and less expensive to purchase birds from reputable dealers and established importers.

Government regulations for imports are becoming increasingly complex, so domestic breeding has become an alternative worthy of serious considera-tion—especially as the availability of certain species, already limited, is likely to worsen.

A Fish and Wildlife official inspects a shipment of blue–fronted Amazons from Argentina.

Acclimating Correctly

Never place new birds with your existing stock, but quarantine them for at least 14 days in a separate cage. During the last few days, the cage can be placed near the cage, show case, or indoor aviary into which the new bird will eventually be introduced. In the case of the garden aviary, the whole cage can be placed inside it, but ensure that it is a warm day. Eventually, let the new birds out among the others. Ensure that seed and water containers are placed in the center of the aviary so that the new birds can easily find them should they be unaware of the location of the permanent sites. Sometimes the existing birds will give involuntary help to the new ones by "showing" them where the feeding and watering sites are. In the quarantine cage it is not necessary to have feed or water dispensers placed on the bars. A dish of seed and a dish of water in the center of the floor is adequate.

Considerations Before You Buy

Birds arriving from other countries require some additional precautions. Males and females should be housed separately in roomy cages. A good choice is a box cage that is well protected on all sides. An infrared lamp about 25 inches (65 cm) away from the front of the cage helps the birds stay healthy—especially those weary after a long, tiring journey. Arrange the setup so the bird can move away from the heat at will.

Unless the birds are weak and need constant heat for a longer period, after two weeks, use of the infrared lamp should be limited to nighttime. The infrared lamp provides enough light if it is left on day and night. Afterwards, I recommend providing a night light (a 4- to 7-watt bulb) so the birds can see to eat and/or drink at night.

Outdoor Aviaries

Newly purchased birds should not be subjected to outside temperatures for 10 to 20 days. When they are accustomed to their new surroundings, acclimated to the temperature, and content, they may—on a calm, sunny morning—be released in the garden aviary. Birds that are acquired in the winter months should never be placed in garden aviaries until the spring, and although birds that are acquired in the spring or summer may be placed in roomy cages in the aviaries during the day, they should be brought indoors at night or on really cold and/or windy days.

Developing the Diet

Almost all finches and small parrots love panicum millet. Provide a dish of the small varieties of millet as well as canary grass seed (or white seed), niger, and grass seeds.

After the birds have been in quarantine for two weeks, start offering them chickweed for green food (see page 53) as well as small amounts of egg food (see page 53). For the first four days, to prevent diarrhea, avoid giving new birds fortified or green food. Sprouted seed, however, is a good addition.

After 10 days, you can also supply insects such as ant pupae, small mealworms, white worms, fruit flies, etc., to chipper, healthy birds. Keep in mind, however, that birds introduced to new kinds of foods are prone to diarrhea. If it occurs, discontinue the new food for several weeks.

For drinking water, provide tap water that has been boiled, cooled, and disinfected. I have had consistent success with fresh, cooled camomile tea. It has a healing quality for mild intestinal and stomach disorders—even those involving diarrhea. Make it fresh twice a day (camomile tea quickly turns sour in warm weather); in the evening, replace it with the disinfected tap water.

Situate drinking cups so droppings cannot fall into the water. Water can also be provided in flat earthenware dishes as long as it is covered with wire mesh to stop birds from bathing in it.

After two weeks, I provide only the tap water at room temperature. In areas with hard water, I suggest using distilled or spring water, which can be purchased at grocery stores.

Because recently arrived birds instinctively search for food on the floor, some feed should be sprinkled on the floor as well as placed in seed dishes hung low in the cage, close to the perches. After they have become accustomed to these arrangements in their new home, this procedure may be abandoned.

Bathing Procedures

Recently imported birds should not bathe for the first two to three weeks—wait until they perch lively and healthy.

Once again, I provide tap water cooled to room temperature mixed with one-third part cooled camomile tea, which also has a healing function in bath water. I add the tea because birds like to drink before they bathe.

After a week, you can omit the tea. If patches of inflamed skin (which can be hidden from view by the feathers) are discovered, they will probably clear up after exposure to the tea.

Considerations Before You Buy

Setting Up the Cage

Scatter sand or grit on the floor of the cage and replace it daily; this will help eliminate intestinal bacteria. New arrivals sometimes ingest too much sand or grit, however. If you find this happening, cover the cage floor with plain paper (not newspaper). Too large an intake of sand or grit can also cause stomach and intestinal disorders.

Keep the cage scrupulously clean and wash all utensils with hot water, disinfecting them daily.

Final Cautions

Watch carefully for watery droppings, which can signal a life-threatening situation. If they are found, take immediate action by adding a 5% to 10% glucose solution to the bird's drinking water. Also, provide some poppy seed in the normal seed mix.

For one to two weeks give oxytetracycline HCL 20% at a dosage of .2 ounces per quart (5 g per liter) of drinking water; it is an excellent antibiotic. Another popular antibiotic is sigmamycine, which is administered at .4 ounce per quart (10 g per liter) of drinking water, for one to two weeks.

The acclimation period takes about a month. Afterwards, the birds should be housed in a roomy aviary or cage.

If birds are kept outdoors, they should not be exposed to temperatures below 71.6°F (22°C). Aviaries should have a protective sleeping coop (a night shelter) with plenty of sleeping boxes. If evenings are chilly, the cages should be moved indoors. In the early spring and fall seasons, recently acclimated birds should not be housed outside at all.

By the way, birds should not be used for breeding until a year after their arrival; it weakens them too much.

Additionally, African and Australian bird species have to adjust to a new succession of seasons—when it is summer there, it is winter here, and vice versa. And recently imported females are more likely to develop egg binding if they haven't had enough exercise during the acclimation period.

Be Informed

To receive bird-related information or to become involved in an important industry activist group, contact: The Pet Industry Joint Advisory Council, 1710 Rhode Island Ave., N.W., 2nd Floor, Washington, DC 20036. Phone: (202) 452-1525.

For more information on government regulations, write to: U.S. Department of Agriculture, Animal and Plant Health Inspection Service, Import/Export Staff, Federal Building, Hyattsville, MD 20782.

Housing, Care, and Management

A golden rule, which is often quoted, but seldom observed, is: first the housing, then the birds! If this rule is followed, then all possible arrangements for housing the new tenants should be made, so that the birds can be introduced directly and without fuss into their new quarters.

Pet birds are extremely adaptable to various forms of housing, providing a few logical rules are followed. In the first place, *birds require adequate light and cannot tolerate drafts:* These two factors must be taken into account by the fancier, if he wishes to have success with birds of any kind.

Indoor Accommodations

Pet birds may be kept in cages, show cases, breeding cages, bird rooms, or indoor aviaries, depending on the available space and the aims and intentions of the enthusiast. No rigid differences can be drawn between the various types of accommodation, but we can say that a cage is an enclosure in which a single bird (or a pair) is kept, whereas an aviary is larger and designed to hold a collection of birds (or, in some cases a breeding pair). There is a smaller version of the garden aviary: the so-called room aviary. In such an enclosure—perhaps in an apartment or in a house where no garden is available—a colorful collection of birds can be kept and bred. A bird room is the entire room of a house, with mesh screens over the windows and a safety porch, but with similar contents (nest boxes, plants in pots, drinking and bathing containers, etc.) to an outdoor aviary. A show case is a cage, usually made from glass, with a solid rear wall (often illustrated with some kind of landscape) and solid side walls; in addition to one or two pairs of birds, such a case is decorated with nonpoisonous house plants (see the list of potentially poisonous plants) in order to create a "natural" habitat. Finally, there is the breeding cage—available in many types from your pet shop—which is totally enclosed except for a

wire grill at the front. Breeding cages are used mainly for the breeding of various small parrots (for example lovebirds), budgerigars, canaries and various Australian grass finches, such as zebra finches, Gouldian finches, red-faced parrot finches, and long-tailed finches, just to name a few.

Some of the More Common Potentially Poisonous House Plants

Amaryllis	(*Amaryllis* species)
Autumn Crocus	(*Colchicum* species)
Azalea	(*Azalea* species)
Balsam Pear	(*Memordica charantia*)
Bird of Paradise	(*Poinciana gilliensii*)
Boxwood	(*Buxus* species)
Caladium	(*Caladium* species)
Castor Bean	(*Ricinus communis*)
Chalice Vine	(*Solandra* species)
Coral Plant	(*Jatropha multifida*)
Daffodil	(*Narcissus* species)
Datura (berries only)	(*Datura* species)
Dieffenbachia	(*Dieffenbachia picta*)
Elephant's Ear	(*Colocasia* species)
Hyacinth	(*Galtonia* species)
Hydrangea	(*Hydrangea macro phylla*)
Japanese Yew	(*Taxus cuspidata*)
Java Beans	(*Phaseolus lunatus* var.)
Lantana	(*Lantana* species)
Lily-of-the-Valley	(*Convallaria majalis*)
Narcissus	(*Narcissus* species)
Nightshade (Deadly, Black, Garden or Woody Nightshade, and Eggplant [all except fruit])	(*Solanaceae*)
Oleander	(*Nerium* species)
Philodendron	(*Philodendron* species)
Rhododendron	(*Rhododendron* species)
Yam Bean	(*Pachyrhisus* erosus)

If you want to get into a new color variation, the easiest way, is to buy a couple of pure-breeding (homozygous) budgies of that color.
Above left and right: an albino and blue parakeet;
Below: yellow, blue, and green parakeets.

Housing, Care, and Management

Some common potentially poisonous houseplants: Top: Caladium (left) and Dieffenbachia (right). Bottom: Azalea (left) and Hyacinth (right). At the first sign of any abnormal bird behavior, consult with your avian veterinarian immediately.

Cages

When acquiring a cage, the first consideration must be the total length. In captivity every bird must have room to fly, not just to spread its wings, so that it may maintain good health. If a bird has insufficient room to spread its wings, this will be a real detriment to its health. A cage which is so small that a bird can jump, in one spring from perch to perch, without using its wings, is really a prison and no home for our feathered friends. Whatever kind of bird is to be kept in a cage, adequate length is much more important than width. An efficient, roomy,

Above left: The peach-faced lovebird is an expert flier. Above right: Gray-cheeked parakeets. In the wild they build their nests in termite mounds and hollows of trees. Below: In 1963, the Dutch ornithologist P. Habats bred the first blue peach-faced lovebird, which eventually became the most common of all the mutations.

and sensible home is what the bird requires, so that the owner can enjoy its splendid color, form, and melodious song.

In the last few years, countless types of cages have been manufactured at home and abroad and brought into the pet trade. Vast improvements in cages have been made in recent times, with such sophistications as sliding floor trays to ease cleaning; strong water and food containers which can be fixed to the cage sides; and well-chromed wires.

The most recent cages for birds are revolutionary in design; instead of the old original metal base, the new bases are cast in solid seamless plexiglass or hard plastic, which is glass clear, or—most recently—brightly colored. The cleaning of these modern cages is very easy, in that the base can be removed by loosening a few clips. The cage and the birds are placed on a sheet of paper and the base can then be cleaned (see page 34). When everything is spotless, and the containers filled with food and water, then the cage may be placed on the base and the clips secured.

As mentioned earlier, the length of the cage is of prime importance. It is best to stick to the following *minimum* sizes:

• For birds the size of a zebra finch or smaller: $19\frac{1}{2}$ × 10 × 12 inches (50 × 25 × 30 cm); this length will also house a pair of small bird species. A cage of the same length, but with a width of 14 inches (35 cm) and a height of 16 inches (40 cm), is suitable for a pair of birds or one bird the size of a canary. Wires must be set 19 gauge—$\frac{1}{2}$ × $\frac{1}{2}$ inch (12.5 × 12.5 mm), no more. The height and width of cages for small finches (waxbills, zebra finches, etc.) are of little importance.
• Cages intended for birds the size of a Pekin robin or a golden-fronted leafbird should have dimensions that are no smaller than $23\frac{1}{2}$ × 14 × 16 inches (60 × 35 × 40 cm).
• Cages for thrushes or similar birds should have minimum dimensions of $31\frac{1}{2}$ × 16 × $19\frac{1}{2}$ inches (80 × 40 × 50 cm).

Housing, Care, and Management

• Cages for budgerigars or lovebirds, as a pair or a single bird: $23\frac{1}{2} \times 12 \times 16$ inches ($60 \times 30 \times 40$ cm). The wire must run horizontally so that the birds can climb. This goes for all cages in which parrots or parakeets are to be kept.
• Cages for form and posture canaries: $23\frac{1}{2} \times 19\frac{1}{2} \times 23\frac{1}{2}$ inches ($60 \times 50 \times 60$ cm).
• Cages for a pair of cockatiels $39\frac{1}{2} \times 23\frac{1}{2} \times 23\frac{1}{2}$ inches ($100 \times 60 \times 60$ cm); for a single bird: $19\frac{1}{2} \times 17\frac{1}{2} \times 17\frac{1}{2}$ inches ($50 \times 45 \times 45$ cm).
• Cages for large parrots, a pair or a single bird: $59 \times 59 \times 63$ inches ($150 \times 150 \times 160$ cm).
• Cages for small parrots (conures, rosellas, etc.): $47 \times 35\frac{1}{2} \times 35\frac{1}{2}$ inches ($120 \times 90 \times 90$ cm).
• Cages for small doves (diamond dove, etc.): $39\frac{1}{2} \times 27\frac{1}{2} \times 19\frac{1}{2}$ inches ($100 \times 70 \times 50$ cm).
• Cages for mynahs and jays: $39\frac{1}{2} \times 21\frac{1}{2} \times 21\frac{1}{2}$ inches ($100 \times 55 \times 55$ cm).

Guidelines for Choosing Wire Mesh

Wire Gauge	Mesh Size	Suitability
19G	$\frac{1}{2} \times \frac{1}{2}$ inch (12.5×12.5 mm)	African finches (wax-bills) and small soft-billed birds
19G	$\frac{1}{2} \times 1$ inch (12.5×25 mm)	Australian finches, budgerigars, Australian grass parakeets, and doves (diamond dove, etc.)
16G	$1\frac{1}{2} \times \frac{1}{2}$ inch (12.5×12.5 mm)	Grass parakeets, love-birds, aratingas conures, and other small parakeets
16G	$\frac{1}{2} \times 1$ inch (12.5×25 mm)	Larger parakeets, my-nahs, thrushes and similar-sized soft-billed birds
14G	1×1 inch (25×25 mm)	Amazons, African grays, dwarf macaws, and similar-sized birds
12G	2×2 inches (50×50 mm)	Cockatoos, large ma-caws, and similar-sized birds

A decorative cage with a "double bottom," the top of which is also constructed of wire grating.

Four rules to keep in mind when buying a bird cage:
• A caged bird must have enough room to move with ease. A caged bird should be able to flap its wings without touching the sides of the cage.
• A cage that is longer in length or width is much better than one that is square.
• A rectangular cage is better than a round one as it offers excellent flying room. A rectangular cage is by far the best housing for any pet bird.
• Tower cages (the narrow, tall type) are impractical; birds are not helicopters—in other words, they don't fly straight up and down.

The bird keeper must not be misled by the little exhibition cages in which birds spend only a couple of days; for technical reasons and reasons of space, they are very small. Remember, however, that these are only temporary shelters!

Cages with a solid back wall are preferable to completely open models. The solid wall will be a protection against drafts and it will give the birds more security. Thus, the so-called breeding cages (totally enclosed except for the cage front) do very well; not only do they prevent the birds from be-

Housing, Care, and Management

Only spacious cages, in which the bird can move about freely, should be purchased; avoid *round* cages as these can make the birds nervous.

coming nervous, they also increase the likelihood of their breeding.

Parrots and parakeets are normally kept in wire cages, while finches and soft-billed birds are kept in enclosed cages (except for the front), made of wood, metal, or hard plastic. Brand-new unpainted cages and show cases, suitable for most bird species, are available in the pet stores. These are usually box models (with a wire or mesh front); all you need to do is check the length and width of the wire. (You don't want any escapees!) These models usually have sliding or hinged doors; the latter are more suitable for parrots, which soon learn to operate a sliding door!

Whenever painting cages, use lead-free paint, as lead compounds can be dangerous to birds. All ready-made cages should come complete with perches, food and drink containers, and an easy-to-operate sliding bottom tray, so that cleaning chores pose no problems.

Show Cases

Show cases of various types are available from avicultural suppliers. Naturally, one can also make one's own. I will be brief on construction details; everybody has different tastes, and available space is also a factor to take into consideration. The majority of show cases have a glass front (although some may have a mesh front, with a glass or plastic

"Cathedral" bird cage from England or the United States, circa 1850. Not a "kind" cage for pet birds!

23

strip at the bottom to prevent feathers and seed, etc., from soiling the floor) and roof lights along the sides or against the mesh (for example, 15-watt fluorescent tubes). The lighting apparatus should not be visible to the observer; it should be concealed behind a roof strip. In addition, you should include a heat lamp for cages placed near windows and doors (beware of drafts!) where the temperature at night can drop drastically. (It is wise to use a thermostat.)

An attractive show case for small birds, such as finches, parakeets (budgerigars), and canaries.

The solid rear wall can be decorated with a nature scene, which should not be too gaudy. It is best to place a sheet of glass which can be removed and cleaned of droppings, etc., against the rear wall. Plants, in pots or boxes, can be used in the show case for further decoration. Naturally, you should take special care with the planting, using only hardy species, and avoiding any with poisonous leaves or fruits. The minimum size for a show case should be $31\frac{1}{2} \times 23\frac{1}{2} \times 19\frac{1}{2}$ inches ($80 \times 60 \times 50$ cm). Such a case would be suitable for three small and tolerant bird couples (African waxbills, for example); for larger birds, such as thrushes, lovebirds, or tana-

gers, this size is suitable for a single pair only.

Should you need to catch birds from the show case, a long-handled, fine-meshed net, which is obtainable in most pet stores (I say at the outset *fine meshed*, otherwise birds are likely to get caught in it) may be used or—and this is much better—wait until the evening when it is almost dark, and you can simply lift the bird off the perch by hand. Various doors, not too small, are necessary at the ends of the show case for easy access. If you catch birds in your hand, do it with great care so that the other birds do not (or barely) notice. Try to avoid causing panic, as birds flying about in the dark will soon injure themselves. If you are not immediately successful in catching the right bird, and panic does ensue, switch on the light immediately so that the birds can quickly find their sleeping places. In such cases it is best to leave the catching until the following night.

A double floor for a show case is highly recommended; the upper one should be removable.

The Box Cage

A bird feels most at ease if kept in a partly enclosed cage: the so-called box cage, a unit in which only the front is covered in mesh, the rest—the three walls, floor, and roof—is totally enclosed. Such a cage must stand in a brightly lit, draft-free spot. Not in full sunlight, as such a cage can, in a short time, become like an oven. Box cages, which are most useful for pairs of birds for breeding, may not fit into the decor of a living room or den.

A box breeding cage for various finches, parakeets, lovebirds and similar–sized birds. Note the sliding tray for easy cleaning.

24

Housing, Care, and Management

An excellent box breeding cage for canaries or parakeets. Note that the two sliding panels that separate the birds can be removed when mating is desired or when chicks must be separated from their parents. The sliding tray at the bottom of the cage facilitates cleaning. On top of this box cage is a show cage; this model is often used for various finch species and parakeets (budgerigars).

T-bar Stand

The T-bar stand consists of a vertical bar set into a heavy base, with a horizontal perch set across the top; on the outer ends of the perch food and water containers are mounted. Under the perch a large circular tray is mounted to catch droppings, seed husks, etc. A T-bar stand is suitable only for a tame parrot or parakeet. Every parrot soon learns where the stand is located and will quickly refrain from flying about the room. At one time, the bird was fastened to the stand by means of a ring on its foot and a chain but fortunately, this practice is now illegal. Be sure that the bird always has something to occupy itself with, for example twigs to gnaw, millet spray to eat, wooden toys to help pass the time, or a honey stick (see page 48) to eat and play with. Sitting on the perch can become boring after a short time and can lead to psychological problems, such as feather picking. Therefore, wooden ladders, bells attached to a stout rope (on which to climb), and other such toys should be available. The

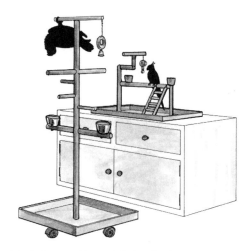

The T-bar stand is used during the day as a temporary release from the cage. The playpen is an assortment of toys, swings, and ladders that can be handcrafted or purchased in most pet stores.

T-bar stand is really a "playground" for parrots and parakeets that would otherwise be kept in cages.

Naturally, the tray and the food and water containers should be cleaned daily. The bar should never be placed in a hall, kitchen, porch, stairway, or other drafty room, or in dark places such as a cellar, garage, or shed.

The Indoor Aviary and the Bird Room

The indoor aviary—an aviary in a room in the house—is popular for keeping and breeding soft-billed birds and delicate finches, as it is easy to keep at a suitable temperature. This is not to say that the indoor aviary is unsuitable for hardier birds, but bear in mind that some species (for example, zebra finches) are better suited to the outdoor aviary. A properly set up indoor aviary can make a truly spectacular addition to the decor of a room. It will also provide an endless source of fascination for you and your guests.

Housing, Care, and Management

The interior of a well-kept bird room.

Many people confuse an indoor aviary with a bird room. The latter is an entire spare room that is used as an aviary. Recently, the indoor aviary has been gaining in popularity and it is possible to buy assembly kits from avicultural suppliers. The bird room is used mainly by specialists to breed Australian grass finches, soft-billed birds, and various canaries.

The Outdoor Aviary

This book cannot provide detailed plans for building an outdoor (or garden) aviary, but a few basic facts can be noted. A garden aviary usually consists of two, sometimes three sections: a shelter, a half-open section (of which the roof is covered with corrugated plastic sheeting or something similar), and an open section, which is normally called "the flight." A two-section aviary is minus the half-open part. Personally, I am of the opinion that a three-section aviary is the most useful.

When you select a good site for your aviary, you are already on the right track. Wherever possible, the front of the aviary should face south. If this is not feasible, then as much as possible should face south, and I would recommend southeast rather than southwest. It is a good idea to have part of the front covered with glass, especially if it does not face south (glass, not mirror; songbirds will stop singing if they can see themselves, and parrots can "fall in love" with their own images!) Another thing to be kept in mind is that the aviary should be situated in an attractive and easily observed part of the garden, preferably with flowers and shrubs both surrounding it and in the background—not so the structure is lost but rather so that it becomes part of the general scene, creating a natural effect.

What materials do you need? I would advise you not to build entirely of wood, especially if you intend to keep parrots or parakeets. The foundation should be made from concrete or brickwork, to which are attached the uprights (if you are *not* keeping parrotlike birds) or metal posts. The foundation wall should extend about 12 to 19½ inches (30 to 50 cm) above ground. The floor of the shelter is set at this height; it is built preferably of concrete or concrete slabs, over which is spread a thick layer of sand. The walls and the roof are best made from tongued and grooved pine boards. You also require wire mesh (see page 22) and some kind of roofing material—tiles, slates, corrugated plastic, fiberglass, wire-reinforced glass, etc. Use narrow posts—the narrower the better as these are less likely to shrink and pull. For mesh, use the common six-sided aviary mesh; if large parrot varieties are to be kept, the preferred type is square-welded wire mesh, which is available in various thicknesses (see page 22). Other more expensive types of woven wire are also available. A gutter and a downspout are usually necessary.

The number of birds you can keep in an outdoor aviary will depend on the amount of available space and on the form and size of the enclosure. You must always beware of overpopulating an aviary; inces-

Housing, Care, and Management

sant squabbling and fighting, particularly over the seed and food containers, will indicate whether you have placed too many birds in the aviary.

Another tip about the design of an outdoor aviary: The main ingredient is the contents and not the frivolity of fancy domes and arches. Design the aviary to fit into the natural atmosphere of the garden. Should this not be possible immediately, plant shrubs, trees, and flowers in the area to complement those that are already in the garden. A special consideration is the height of a garden avi-

ary. Never build one which is too low; a height of 6½ to 8¼ feet (2–2½ m) should be the minimum for aesthetic appeal.

The Shelter

This can be built from timber, metal, bricks, etc. It is recommended that the inside of the shelter be lined and insulated, to prevent excessive cold and drafts. The majority of acclimated tropical birds can tolerate a considerable amount of frost, but damp-

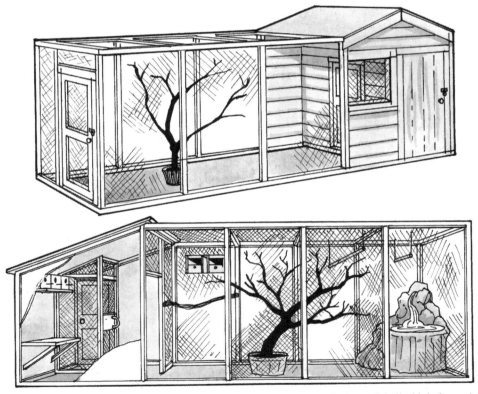

Two small garden aviaries suitable for canaries (top), or small and medium-sized finches and similar birds (bottom). Note the safety porches in both night shelters, which are an essential requirement to prevent the birds from escaping.

Housing, Care, and Management

A roomy double flight outdoor aviary with safety porch, for various small psittacines, such as lovebirds, conures, rosellas, and grass parakeets.

ness and drafts can be killers for the residents of a garden aviary. Although it is essential to keep the shelter dry and free of drafts, good ventilation is also important to keep birds in good condition. Such ventilation can be provided by the installation of adjustable vents in the walls.

It is important to run a wire brush over the new aviary mesh. This removes any excess zinc (from the galvanizing process) which can be very dangerous to your birds.

The Flight

If the flight is not mounted on a solid concrete floor (this is highly recommended for parrotlike birds, in order to keep a check on worm infestation), then take great care to include measures for controlling rats and mice. At the outset, ensure that the mesh is buried in the ground to a depth of at least 8 inches (20 cm) to prevent vermin from burrowing in from the outside. If possible, it is best to set the mesh *into* concrete, so that it does not rip. The mesh can be given a coat of flat nonpoisonous, black paint,

which eliminates the glare of the galvanizing and enables one to see the contents of the aviary more clearly. All timber and metal work should be protected with nonpoisonous preservatives, which obviously should be allowed to dry thoroughly before any birds are introduced.

Plants

Various plants may be included in a garden aviary to render it more natural looking. Interestingly shaped dead tree trunks and branches (willow, for example) can also be used to enhance the scene, especially if you keep parrotlike birds, which will soon destroy any living plants. Plants around the garden aviary should be varieties that attract in-

Above left: The Alexandrine parakeet is an intelligent bird; it can even be taught to speak.
Above right: Young male red-rumped parakeet.
Bottom left: The plum-headed parakeet from India.
Below right: Bourke's parakeets make excellent foster parents for memebers of the genus *Psephotus*.

28

Housing, Care, and Management

A single garden aviary, suitable for lovebirds, parakeets (budgerigars), canaries and finches. Note the container drawer, which can be pushed inside the aviary when filled with treats or daily seed mixtures.

sects, that will then enter the aviary and provide additional food and pleasure for the birds.

The following plants are suitable for *inside* the garden aviary:

• American Arbor Vitae (*Thuja occidentalis*). This is a good hedge, especially for a community aviary of small tropical birds.
• Australian Pine (*Pinus nigra*). Many birds like to build their nests in pines, especially if you help them get started with a base of woven rope, or the like, placed between the branches or in a fork.
• Bamboo (*Sinarundinaria*). Mannikins and other small finches whose nails tend to grow fast like to

Above left: The crimson rosella or pennant lives in pairs or in groups and spend a lot of time on the ground.
Above right: The splendid grass parakeet inhabits dry scrubland and is rare in the wild.
Below left: Mitchell's lorikeets from Bali and Lombok, were first bred by Clifford Smith in 1972 (England).
Below right: Nanday parakeets can be kept with finches.

frequent bamboo.
• Beech (*Fagus sylvatica*). This tree can provide needed shade.
• Boxwood, Common (*Buxus sempervirens*). Many birds like to build nests in this evergreen, particularly finches and weavers.
• Broom (*Sarothamnus scoperius*). Hollow the sheaf out a little, and the birds will love to build nests in it.
• Buddleia (*Buddleia davidii*). Young plants are worth planting as birds like them for nest building, for resting, or for overnight shelter.
• Climbing Rose (*Rosa multiflora*). The plant makes an unusually good hedge and therefore is quite suited to a roomy garden aviary. Many varieties of roses are quite susceptible to aphids, which provide a special feast for many birds.
• *Cotoneaster*. The shrub produces pitted red fruits that are a treat for fruit-eating birds, particularly thrushes and larger finch species.
• English Hawthorn (*Crataegus monigyna*). This low, deciduous shrub has a tight network of

branches that many birds like to use for nesting.

• English Holly (*Ilex aquifolium*). This evergreen is extremely well suited to all types of outdoor aviaries except for aviaries for parrotlike birds, thrushes, and the like.

• European Elderberry (*Sambucus nigra*). The black berries are readily eaten by all types of birds; another important characteristic is that elderberry attracts aphids.

• European Hornbeam (*Carpinus betulus*). This is truly an ideal plant for the aviary, especially because birds love to nest in it.

• European Larch (*Larix decidua*). This tree is suited to aviaries, including those with poor soil.

• Ivy (*Hedera helix*). Excellent for aviaries with tropical finches as they will nest in it, especially if some rope is wound between the branches to provide a nesting base.

• Japanese Spirea (*Spirea japonica*). This shrub is considered an ideal plant for the aviary because it has a thickly branched type of growth.

• Juniper (*Juniperus communis*). The less varied forms of the bush are best for the aviary. Birds often build nests in it, or use it to simply spend the night.

• Oriental (or Chinese) Cedar (*Thuja orientalis*). Birds enjoy nesting in this tree, particularly if several (at least three) are planted close together, forming a large, interlocking hedge. Breeding birds feel safe and secluded there.

• Privet, Common (*Liguster vulgare*). Many large parakeets, cocktiels, canaries, and large finches like to eat the leaves and/or buds, which are a good supplement to their regular diet. Tropical birds, and small finches in particular, consider this plant an ideal location for breeding, and canaries and large finches like to spend time in this plant on sunny days.

• Red Ribes (*Ribes sanguinen*). This shrub is highly recommended as an aviary plant, if only for its bright red berries.

• Willow (*Salix*). There are many species of willow, and any of them can serve as an aviary plant. They can be bushes or trees. If you keep parrots and/or

Some of the More Common Potentially Poisonous Outdoor Plants

American Yew	(*Taxus canadensis*)
Baneberry	(*Actaea* species)
Bittersweet Nightshade	(*Solanum dulcamara*)
Black Locust	(*Robinia pseudoacacia*)
Bloodroot	(*Sanguinario* species)
Buckthorn	(*Rhamnus* species)
Buttercup	(*Ranunculus* species)
Calla Lily	(*Zantedeschia aethiopica*)
Cherry Tree	(*Prunus* species)
Christmas Candle	(*Pedilanthus tithymaloides*)
Clematis	(*Clematis* species)
Cowslip	(*Caltha* species)
Daphne	(*Daphne* species)
English Holly	(*Ilex aquifolium*). For aviaries with parrotlike birds, thrushes, etc.
English Yew	(*Taxus baccata*)
Golden Chain or Laburnum	(*Laburnum anagyroides*)
Henbane	(*Hyoscyamus niger*)
Hemlock	(*Conium maculatum*)
Honey Locust	(*Gleditsia triacathos*)
Horse Chestnut	(*Aesculus* species)
Indian Turnip	(*Arisaema triphyllum*)
Iris	(*Iris* species)
Jack-in-the-Pulpit	(*Arisaema triphyllum*)
Jimsonweed	(*Datura* species)
Larkspur	(*Delphinium* species)
Locoweed	(*Astragalus mollissimus*)
Lords and Ladies	(*Arum* species)
May apple	(*Podophyllum* species)
Mistletoe (only the berries)	(*Santalales* species)
Monkshood	(*Aconitum* species)
Morning Glory	(*Ipomoea* species)
Mountain Laurel	(*Kalmia latifolia*)
Nutmeg	(*Myristica fragrans*)
Pokeweed	(*Phytolacca amaricana*)
Rhubarb	(*Rheum rhaponticum*)
Rosary Peas	(*Abrus precatorius*)
Snowdrop	(*Galanthus nivalis*)
Snowflake	(*Leucoium vernum*)
Sweet Pea	(*Lathyrus latifolius*)
Tobacco	(*Nicotiana* species)
Water Hemlock	(*Cicuta maculata*)
Western Yew	(*Taxus breviflora*)

parakeets in particular, you should not pass up the opportunity to place a willow in the aviary—even a dead stump will do. Hookbills just love to hack and gnaw at the wood, and they like the bark. Many species, such as lovebirds (*Agapornidae*), use willow bark for constructing their nests. Willow thrives in moist, loose soil, and needs to be trimmed. If you keep hookbills, you should furnish some fresh-cut willow branches every day. Many finches and weavers like to nest in willow bushes.

Accessories

Perches

Commercial perches are made from hard wood—for example, beech—and should not be too narrow. Stick to the following rule: Perches on which the feet can just grip are the best. In other words, the bird should be able to sit on the perch so that its toes cannot grip all the way around. If the perch is too thin, the toes are not protected by the belly feathers of the resting bird. During the winter months birds are especially subject to frostbite of the toes. Smooth perches can also pose a problem. The bird's feet cannot get a good grip. One should roughen a smooth perch with a file or with sandpaper. There are two kinds of perches: round perches that are somewhat flattened along the top, so that the feet are more comfortable and the excessive growth of the claws is retarded; and a perch that is square, but with the four edges somewhat rounded—this is easy to do with a file. I personally recommend this second type; birds will rest much better on such perches.

When we speak of hard wood, bear in mind that in less than no time, parrots will decimate soft wood. In addition, soft wood is an ideal hiding place for bacteria, parasitic insects, and other pests.

In order to divert parrotlike birds from gnawing on perches, give them something else more attractive to keep them occupied—for example: apple, plum, and nut twigs; willow and elder. The twigs

Hookbills love to hack and gnaw at willow stumps and branches, and they like the bark.

should be kept in a cool place for about two weeks to allow them to dry.

In roomy cages and in aviaries, you can install perches of various thicknesses, including a variety of fixed and swinging branches. Natural plants (if present) will also provide resting places. Most perches should be placed in the shelter, so that the birds are encouraged to spend the night protected. When birds are accustomed to sleeping in the shelter, be careful not to disturb them at night during the winter months. Perches should be placed as high as possible (and preferably higher in the shelter than in the flight) as most bird species like to sleep in the highest place available. For many South American parakeets, it is recommended that a plank be installed around the upper wall of the shelter, about 16 inches (40 cm) from the ceiling. Aratinga species, for example, will use such a shelf in preference to a standard perch. Extra climbing branches should also be provided in the shelter and in the outside flight as plants would not last long otherwise.

Housing, Care, and Management

In cages, the perches are best placed before the food and water containers. At least one perch should be placed high in the cage, so that the birds have the choice of an elevated sleeping place. Do not stuff the cage with perches; room for free movement must be available. Also, perches should not be placed above each other; otherwise the droppings of the upper birds will soil the plumage of the lower. Perches should not be covered with sandpaper. As Dr. R. Dean Axelson rightly says: "Making a bird stand on a sandpaper-covered perch is comparable to making someone walk along on a gravel road in bare feet."

Sand in the Floor Tray

A well-constructed cage should have a sliding floor tray, which helps to keep cleaning chores easy. Some cages have a top that can be separated from the bottom (see page 21). The best way to prepare the floor of the cage is to lay neatly folded, thick paper (such as grocery bags) on it. Do not use newspaper, as some birds—especially parrots—will gnaw at it and the printing ink can be poisonous. On top of the paper, spread a thick (approximately 1 inch [2 cm]) layer of shell sand, mixed with grit. Such "bird sand" is available in various brands from avicultural suppliers. To stop sand from falling out of the cage, a 4-inch (10-cm) border of clear plastic is placed around the bottom of the cage; usually this is already part of the cage, but if not, then you should install it yourself.

Food and Water Dishes

Food and water dishes, made from a sturdy, nontoxic material, must be placed where the droppings of birds cannot fall into them from perches, etc. They must also be easy to remove from the cage/aviary, so that they can be regularly cleaned, disinfected, and refilled. Food dishes must be thoroughly dry before use. In aviaries you can use automatic food dispensers and shallow water dishes which are available from avicultural suppliers. Several cuttle-

Various essential food and water containers for small to medium–sized birds. Top left: A shallow commercial birdbath that can be attached to the cage.

Keeping the birds' utensils scrupulously clean and disinfected (which means destroying infective agents like bacteria, viruses, and fungi) will certainly help decrease the possibility of transmitting diseases.

34

Housing, Care, and Management

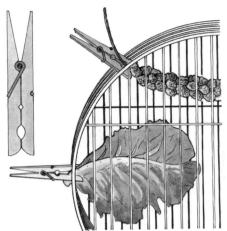

Wooden clothespins are helpful for clamping "treats," such as greens and millet sprays, to the trellis or mesh of cage or aviary.

bones in the cage or aviary are not a luxury, but a necessity; they provide the birds with necessary minerals and help them keep their beaks in good shape. Mineral blocks are also useful for this purpose and are available, with holding brackets, from pet dealers.

Decorative Clips

In the last few years, it has been possible to obtain oversized decorative spring clips about 6 inches (15 cm) in length, from supermarkets, gift shops, and department stores. These are normally used to hold letters, bills, and so forth. Such clips can be very useful to bird fanciers. For example, they can be used to hold open cage doors; to hold green food, toys, and—let us not forget—millet sprays and strips of carrot. The clip can even be used as a "perch," as it can be fixed almost anywhere. Such a clip can also be used in the aviary; for example, for holding twigs and greens to the mesh or between nest boxes; or for holding sisal rope on which the birds like to climb (an excellent therapy

for boredom). There are many other uses for these clips.

Toys

Many parrotlike birds, particularly the smaller species, like to play with various toys. There is a

Strong and durable but *safe* toys help satisfy the parrot's instinct for chewing. There are toys available for all kinds of pet birds. From left to right: bell, lava stone, rawhide chewie, and wooden sticks and bell. In the parrot's claws: a rawhide chew and a flavored and scented nylon ring.

wide choice for birds and we can always provide them with something. Toys are especially valuable for parrots that have to spend many hours alone, to keep them busy and prevent boredom. Birds that are bored will start screaming, or may start plucking their feathers or develop some other unpleasant habit. Bells, swings, ladders, chains, ropes, etc., are all useful. With chains, ensure that the links are large enough to prevent accidents, such as catching the bird's toes. I have noticed that larger parrots especially are fascinated with a key ring (and keys) or a metal spoon. Mirrors and other shiny objects are appreciated by all parrotlike birds. We must be careful, however, that larger birds cannot break the mirrors. Rubber and soft plastic toys are dangerous and should not be given under any circumstances.

Ideal objects are blocks of hard wood, fresh bark-covered tree branches, rawhide, raw vegetables (especially carrots and potatoes), banana skins, dried gourds, coconut shells, seashells, etc. Remember that not all toys will necessarily be accepted right away; it can take several days before the birds will begin to play with them. The various toys must be thoroughly cleaned and sterilized at regular intervals.

Environmental Considerations

Temperature and Humidity

Most birds are really efficiently protected by their plumage, and even tropical birds can tolerate low temperatures. Once acclimated, most birds can

Aviaries with mesh bottoms through which droppings and uneaten food can pass, are very sanitary, and will help prevent bird diseases.

A large garden aviary, consisting of single-pair pens (runs). This type of housing is excellent for breeding various color mutations of cockatiels and lovebirds, and for Australian and South American parakeets.

tolerate temperatures as low as 15° to 20°F (–9.5° to –6.7°C), provided they are not affected by drafts and dampness. The humidity in an ideal environment should be around 40% to 50%. Experiments have proven that birds can better tolerate excessive humidity (for example, readings greater than 50%) than excessive dryness. However, outside of the breeding season, birds can tolerate a humidity of around 30%. During the breeding period, such a low reading is dangerous—the eggs can dry out, or the membranes can become tough and hard, so that the young birds find it impossible to hatch. A general rule is that for birds to feel most comfortable, they should be kept in a moderately warm and not too humid environment. Once more, it should be said with emphasis, draft is the greatest enemy of all birds.

Artificial Light

We know that natural light is essential for the good health of birds. Artificial light alone is sufficient, but if Vita-Lite fluorescent tubes (available in various lengths from better pet stores) are used, the light rays from these come very close to natural daylight. Birds need ultraviolet light to build up body cholesterol and convert it to provitamin D_3. The birds instinctively know what to do. As soon as they have a chance to sun themselves, they spread their wings and take a complete sunbath. Even if they can't sit in the sun, they tend to roost in the lightest places. That is why I recommend a good fluorescent light for indoor bird facilities.

Radio and Television

Birds that have to spend many hours alone in the house will appreciate listening to music. A radio is therefore useful. Find a station which plays peaceful, soft music. However, if you like to have your stereo turned up loud, ensure that it is kept well away from any birds. Loud music will make the birds restless and stressed.

The same can be true of television, which brings the added danger of cathode rays. Finally, TV emits high notes, which we cannot hear, but which are perceived by birds. Therefore, never place a cage on a television set or in its immediate vicinity. It is also best to cover the cage with a cloth when you are watching TV in the evening. A bird should have a minimum of 10 to 12 hours rest each night, and if you stay up to watch late programs, bear in mind that your feathered friends will suffer a lack of sleep.

Air Pollution

Bird cages should never be situated where people smoke heavily; birds are very sensitive. Gas and cooking fumes can also be unhealthy and the fumes of overheated Teflon pans are toxic to birds! The same goes for paint. If you wish to paint a room, first move the cage elsewhere and do not return it to its original spot for at least five days after the painting is finished. Care should also be taken in the use of deodorizing sprays, as well as insecticides,

aerosols, and pest strips. The last are thought to be harmless to birds but it has been proven that they are not altogether harmless. If they are to be used to control parasites, etc., in bird rooms, it is recommended that they be installed for 24 hours, removed for another 24 hours, and installed again; and so on.

Other Pets

If you keep birds, it is highly dangerous to keep a cat as well. Dogs can also make birds nervous by their activity, but a dog can usually be taught to leave birds alone. It is recommended that your pets all be "introduced" to each other, but a careful eye should always be kept on their reactions, particularly during the first weeks.

Letting Birds Fly Free

If you want to let parrots out in the living room or den (and it is recommended you do so for a few hours each day!), then you must first ensure that all doors and windows are well closed, that drapes are

A cage cover at night provides added warmth and security. It sometimes even helps to quiet a noisy bird.

pulled shut (to prevent birds from flying against the glass, which could result in a broken wing, leg, or even neck), that open fireplaces are protected with a fine-meshed guard, and that all electrical apparatuses and ovens are turned off. If during warm days you use a ventilator, then you must ensure that the power plug is efficiently guarded, so that the birds cannot get at it. Houseplants and cut flowers should be removed from the room, as parrots are especially curious and will want to "inspect" them. Not only will your plants be damaged but there is a danger that the bird will be poisoned (see page 18). Cacti can, in addition, cause wounds! Alternatively, the plants can be protected under plastic covers, but be careful that the birds do not gnaw the plastic. If two or more rooms are available for free flight, be sure that birds have not perched on an open door before you close it. Also, make certain that the door can't swing shut itself or be blown closed. And beware of open basins, toilets, and tubs in which birds may drown.

Summer Months

During the higher temperatures of the summer months, it is possible that food, green food, and fruit will quickly go bad. Higher temperatures encourage many pests to breed more rapidly, and bacteria will grow more profusely. Therefore a daily inspection and scrupulous cleanliness are essential. It is recommended that birds that have spent the greater part of the year indoors be given the opportunity to enjoy fresh air in the spring and summer—the more the better. Do not place the cage in the direct sun (there is the possibility of sunstroke) but in a semishaded spot, safe from cats, dogs, and other bird enemies. If you have cats yourself, or if they roam around the area, then a constant watch should be kept. Many cats have made "kills" when the bird fancier was not watching.

If you keep your eyes open, then it is possible to stand the cage on the grass with the bottom tray removed. The birds will have great fun running around on the grass; towards midday you can spray

Psittacines like to take a "shower" under the dripping tap of your kitchen, especially during the warmest time of the day. They also like the fine mist (not a powerful water stream) from a plant sprayer. Don't use one that previously has contained cleaning solutions, pesticides, herbicides, insecticides, or other harmful liquids!

the grass with water if it is a really warm summer's day. The birds will be able to bathe in the wet grass.

Basic Grooming

Bathing

Many kinds of parrots like to roll in wet grass or to sit on the edge of a water container and take a "shower" by dipping their heads quickly in the water and throwing it all over their bodies. A hand-

Cockatiels are at home in the urban areas of Australia as well as in savannah and grassland. They are graceful and peaceable birds that are willing to breed in a roomy cage or garden aviary. There are beautiful color mutations.

ful of wet grass on the floor of the cage, or a piece of wet turf will be really appreciated by parrotlike birds. For finchlike birds, there is the well-known type of bath which can be mounted in the entrance of the cage. In aviaries, shallow dishes can be used. Parrots that are regularly let out of their cages will sooner or later discover the dripping tap in the kitchen (budgerigars and lovebirds especially). Larger parrots love to be sprayed with lukewarm water; a plant atomizer is useful for this.

Claw and Beak Trimming

For trimming beak or nails, clipping wings, or administering medicines, the correct procedure is as follows:

1. Plan ahead. Have everything you need ready before you catch the bird. Remove utensils, toys, and perches which can be used by the bird to hide behind. Wear thick leather gloves when handling medium or large psittacines, as their bite can be painful—macaws, for example, have enough "beak power" to amputate a finger! But even the bite of a cockatiel, lovebird, or budgerigar may hurt.

2. Handle birds gently and firmly so they won't escape. Because birds don't have a diaphragm, their breathing depends on the expansion and contraction of the *chest wall*. If the bird is not restrained with its breast free, death by suffocation is likely to occur—in other words *never* rest your hand on a bird's chest.

3. Work quickly to avoid or minimize stress and overheating.

4. Use a thin cloth or paper towel for small birds (finches, cockatiels) and a bathroom towel for

Above left: The Senegal parrot lives in open forest, woodland, and farmland in western Africa.
Above right: In the wild, the African gray parrots sleep during the night in tall trees.
Below: Amazon parrots are usually excellent pets and good talkers, especially when purchsed young.
Left: Bodin's amazon, right: Cuban amazon.

Trimming claws. Be careful not to cut the part that is supplied with blood ("quick"), but if the nail does start to bleed, a moistened styptic pencil, silver nitrate, iron subsulfate, or a liquid coagulant should be applied to the bleeding end. Note the proper restraining method, and compare this with the drawings on page 58.

medium and large birds, especially psittacines. Grasp the bird from behind with your toweled hand, and remove it from its cage. Then position it in the towel resting in the cupped palm of your hand, placing the thumb on one side of the head, and the other fingers on the opposite side. The other hand is free for the required treatment. A large psittacine or other bird species is caught from behind by throwing a towel over the animal. Grasp the bird in your cupped hand with the fingers positioned as indicated above, and try to slide the index finger over the top of the head. With the free hand wrap the towel completely around the bird's body, and scoop it up; the free hand should rest gently but firmly over the upper part of the legs and, if necessary, the bird can be cradled between your forearm and abdomen; then uncover the bird's head. It is advisable that you recruit a second person assist you with the required treatment.

Feeding

What Should You Feed Cage and Aviary Birds?

This is a question which is not asked often enough. Those who do think about it do not give enough attention to the foremost vital needs of a pet bird or to the fact that every species has its own specific demands. It is not enough just to offer a variety of seed to a seedeater, song seed to a canary, or millet to small tropical birds. The feeding problem for birds is very complicated, particularly with regard to seedeaters.

We must first consider that a seedeater does not necessarily eat seeds exclusively. It will also take green food, fruit, and sometimes a large variety of insects, especially during the breeding season. Finches, for example, will eat a large quantity of insects during this time, particularly caterpillars. In fact, in the early stages, the young are reared almost exclusively on such food.

In general, we can surmise that wild birds have a greater variety of food than captive specimens.

In the wild, birds take mainly unripe seeds. *We* usually offer ripe and dried seeds. This is one of the main dangers in feeding. In the first place, you should ensure that there is a variety. Do not offer just rape and canary seeds to canaries, or millet to small tropical birds. A great variety of seeds is essential, but half-ripe weed seeds are also highly recommended for their high vitamin content.

Always ensure that the seed you purchase is not too old. You may ask: How can I tell how old the seed is? In the first place, purchase from a reputable supplier. You can also test it yourself. Old seed loses its germination strength. Fresh seed should germinate in three to four days.

Germinated Seed

Nearly all birds appreciate germinated seed and, when it is offered, they are likely to ignore all other available food. Germinated seed is rich in vitamins A and E, essential parts of the diet. During the soaking period, prior to germination, the starch in the seed changes into sugar (dextrin). Be careful not to soak the seed for too long, as this could lead to the sugar content turning into alcohol by fermentation. Fermentation in the crop of a bird often leads to sickness such as crop swelling, and can be very dangerous.

Canaries and finches are especially keen on germinated seed and, during the rearing of the young, they are likely to ignore egg and rearing food (see page 53), to the detriment of the offspring. Therefore, germinated seed should be given only in small quantities as a supplement to the main diet and not in place of it. It can be mixed with soft and/ or rearing food, a method which I have found satisfactory.

Take the following seeds in similar amounts:

• Rape seed
• Radish seed
• Lettuce seed
• Mung beans
• White milo seed
• Red milo seed

When all these seeds are fresh, germination should take place at the same time when they are mixed together. Take the following steps:

• Soak the seed in a good quantity of lukewarm water for about 12 hours.
• Rinse the seeds many times in running water, preferably in a stainless-steel sieve.
• Shake the seeds free from the bottom of the sieve and then allow the water to drain off.
• Cover the sieve with a moist cloth and stand it in a warm place.
• Shake and rinse the seed regularly in order to prevent fermentation.
• After 24 hours the shoots will appear.
• Clean the sieve thoroughly after use.

Feeding

Weed Seeds

By weed seeds we mean all those suitable, half-ripe seeds that can be collected from the wild. This does not mean only grass seeds but also those we can grow ourselves. We also refer to the seeds of normal bird food, which we can sow in the garden and allow to grow and in turn go to seed. Millet and canary-grass seed are especially suitable.

Hand–feeding a canary fledgling.

Millet should not be sown too densely. It is best to sow it at the end of April or the beginning of May in a seed box covered with a sheet of glass, and later to set out the young seedlings in the garden. It is advisable to plant them in rows with the plants 4 inches (10 cm) apart and with 6 to 8½ inches (15–20 cm) between the rows. In fertile soil and with plenty of sun, they will grow well and may reach 40 inches (1 meter) in height. Soon the flowers will form, then the sprays, and it will be easy to see when they are ready, usually by August. By this time they will be ideal for feeding to the birds and their young—which will then ignore all other food!

Canary-grass seed can also be grown in this manner, but there is no need to distance the plants so far apart. Canary-grass seed does not form sprays but clusters. You cannot put a better food before your seedeaters! (See page 45.)

In addition, seeding grasses may be collected during the whole summer. These should not be collected near highly trafficked roads, as they could be polluted with vehicle fumes which could be dangerous to your birds. Also, do not collect grass from orchards where the trees have been treated with insecticides or you are again likely to lose irreplaceable birds.

The seeds of shepherd's purse, thistle, and even reeds are eagerly eaten by birds—they are usually very rich in vitamins and minerals.

Seed for Canaries

Here you must distinguish between song and color canaries, or even more accurately, between caged canaries and those that are kept in an aviary; there is a great difference. Aviary birds use much more energy and have to withstand greater climatic fluctuations than their caged counterparts.

You must be sure that the diet you offer is nutritious and has sufficient calories—enough for the correct functioning of the bird's metabolism, depending on where it is housed. A bird kept in a small cage can get by with a much lighter diet than a similar bird in an aviary. You must also ensure that the food you give contains sufficient amounts of fats, carbohydrates, protein, minerals, and vitamins. Consider carefully the use of vitamin preparations. It has been said that "enough is as good as a feast." This is especially true of vitamins. Since competent nutritionists have already worked out the dietary qualities of various seeds and their usefulness, supplementary vitamins may not be necessary.

A seed mix containing appropriate amounts of fresh seeds is of great value, especially in an aviary containing only canaries. Sometimes, particular birds will pick out their favorite seeds and discard the others. This should not cause concern, as the other canaries will eat them.

Feeding

The following is an example of a balanced seed mixture:

Canary-grass seed (white seed)	30%
Rape seed	25%
Yellow millet	15%
White millet	5%
Red millet	5%
Broken oats	5%
Niger/thistle seed	5%
Poppy seed (maw seed)	4%
White lettuce seed	2%
Linseed (flax)	2%
Hemp (if available) or teazle	2%

This mixture is for birds that have room to fly and require a lot of energy; therefore a high calorie diet is given. Birds in cages are a different matter altogether. Whether the cage is large or small does not make much difference. Caged canaries are usually kept especially for their song. Such birds must definitely not be allowed to get fat, otherwise there will be no song. It is best to give such birds mostly canary-grass seed (30%), and especially rape seed (70%). That this diet may be a little inadequate should be obvious. Therefore daily add a small quantity of different seeds as a supplement. I would like to call this second seed mixture "supplemental seed diet"; supply one-half teaspoon of it daily. This supplement can be mixed as follows:

Canary-grass seed	50%
Oats (whole)	20%
Niger seed	15%
White lettuce	5%
Poppy seed	4%
Plantain seed	2%
Flax	2%
Hemp and/or teazle	2%

In the making of these two mixtures an obvious distinction has been made between the song canary, which spends its whole life in the house, and the roller canary which, at end of October or beginning of November, is brought indoors from the aviary to enable the fancier to select the best specimens for breeding in the spring. These latter birds do not spend their entire lives in a small cage and must have a substantial diet. With rollers, the supplemental diet helps to stimulate their song, when the amount of it given is increased. If the song loses its power, then broken hemp can be added to this mixture. As far as feeding goes, the breeder of rollers has the song of his birds partly in his own hands. If the birds have a song that is beautiful, deep, but too soft, then he must withdraw the egg food and give more of the supplemental diet.

Remember that the song becomes too sharp from too much canary-grass seed or too many oats, that hemp stimulates the song, while poppy seed makes the bird slower.

When canaries are placed in breeding cages, a very varied seed menu is essential. It is best to give the same mixture as is offered in the aviary, as described above.

Canaries are not kept in the best condition with seeds alone. See page 53 and following for green food, fruit, grit, cuttlefish bone, etc.

Seed for Tropical Birds

Exotic birds pose a different problem from canaries. With canaries it depends on whether we have cage or aviary specimens, but with exotics it is a matter of the *species*, as we have large and small exotics. We are talking here about seed-eating exotics, not about parrotlike birds.

The small exotics such as red avadavats and zebra finches, have different requirements from weavers and whydahs, while these require a different menu from cardinals, doves, and quail. Often the country of origin and the "mode of life" are important. It is obvious that quails and doves, which seek their food on the ground, eat different seeds

Feeding

Average Composition of Some Commonly Used Seeds for Pet Birds

Seeds	Moisture (%)	Protein (%)	Fat (%)	Fiber (%)	Ca (%)	P (%)	Ash (%)	Carbo-hydrates (%)
Common millet (*Panicum miliaceum*)	9.2	13.1	3.3	9.1	0.03	0.4	4.1	59.7
Spray millet (*Setaria italica*)	12.5	15.0	6.1	11.2	0.03	0.32	6.0	60.1
Canary-grass seed (*Phalaris canariensis*)	15.1	13.7	4.1	21.3	0.05	0.55	10.0	56.2
Hullet oats (*Avena sativa*)	10.0	12.1	4.4	12.0	0.09	0.33	3.4	64.3
Niger seed (*Guizotia abyssinica*)	7.0	20.0	43.2	14.3	0.43	0.65	3.5	12.0
Flax seed (*Linum usitatissiumum*)	7.1	24.2	37.0	6.3	0.23	0.66	4.1	20.0
Sunflower seed (*Helianthus annuus*)	7.1	15.2	28.3	29.1	0.18	0.45	3.2	17.5
Milo (*Andropogon sorghum*)	12.5	12.1	3.6	2.4	0.03	0.27	1.9	69.0
Safflower (*Carthamus tinctorius*)	7.2	14.3	28.0	31.2	—	—	3.0	16.5

from the exotics that live in rice or reed fields. Luckily, most exotics are rather easy boarders and are soon accustomed to strange surroundings and diets. In general, we can make do with two mixtures, one for small and one for large exotics. I consider small exotics to be such bird species as zebra finches, waxbills, and Bengalese. By large exotics I mean quail, doves, cardinals, weavers, whydahs, java sparrows, etc. An excellent basic diet for small finches is:

Yellow millet	40%
White millet	25%
Red millet	15%
Canary-grass seed	15%
Rape seed	5%

With the larger exotics, feeding can be more difficult. Among these are species that require special seeds, but which cannot have them in excessive quantities or they will soon become too fat. The larger exotics and ground birds (quail, doves) require the following:

Yellow millet	45%
White millet	25%
Canary-grass seed	25%
Rape seed	5%

A good supplemental seed diet (daily, in separate cups) for finches, quail, and small doves is:

Teazle	15%
Sunflower seed (small)	15%
Flax	15%
Niger seed	15%
Anise (aniseed)	15%
Sesame seed	10%
Oats (groats or hulled)	10%
Poppy seed	5%

Feeding

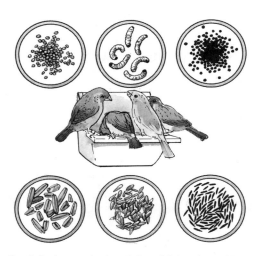

Small finches require (top, left to right) various millets, live food, and rape seed, as well as (bottom, left to right) cracked oats, canary-grass seed (also called white seed), and niger seed.

This supplemental diet should be fed daily as "strewn feed" for doves and quail. Cardinals are fond of a daily ration of small sunflower seed and hemp, but it must be remembered that both seeds are extremely fattening and must be fed sparingly. Ground birds are happy to receive an extra ration of poppy seed, also best strewn over the ground.

You can give all tropical seedeaters a treat by providing them regularly with millet spray, which can be freely suspended in the aviary. This is a delight for the smaller exotics as well as the parakeets which eagerly attack the sprays. Ground birds also get their ration by eating the fallen seeds. Apart from providing the birds with exercise and amusement, millet seeds from the spray are rich in vitamins, making it an extremely useful food.

With these seed mixes, you can keep your exotic birds in prime condition year in and year out, but do not forget to provide supplementary fruit and green food, cuttlefish bone, etc. (see pages 52 and 53).

Seed for Parakeets

Like canaries, parakeets are among the most popular of cage and aviary birds. These birds have an advantage over canaries in that their diet is somewhat simpler and, in addition, they are very sociable birds, especially if kept in pairs or raised by hand.

Although parakeet feeding is simpler, this does not mean to say that you should give them any kind of seed. A conscientious aviculturist will always ensure that his birds receive the best and, in so doing, will see that they remain in prime condition. In addition, we should not forget the enormous satisfaction we gain when our birds willingly start to breed.

As with exotic birds, small parrotlike birds should be given two mixtures, as they can be divided into two groups: on the one side the budgerigars (parakeets, for the American fancier) in all their varieties, and the lovebirds; on the other, the rosellas, cockatiels, gray cheeks, nandays, bee bees, conures, and half-moon parrots, to name just a few.

For the smaller species, make a mixture of:

Canary-grass seed	30%
Yellow millet	20%
Red millet	20%
White millet	20%
Chopped oat groats	10%

For the larger parakeets, the mixture is almost identical:

Canary-grass seed	30%
Yellow millet	20%
Red millet	15%
White millet	15%
Chopped oat groats	10%
Sunflower seed (small)	10%

As a supplemental daily seed mix for both groups, the mixture is:

46

Feeding

Teazle	20%
Anise	20%
Rape seed	10%
Sesame seed	10%
Niger seed	10%
Flax	10%
Milo	10%
Safflower	10%

In addition to the seed menus, larger parakeets may be given a few shelled peanuts on a daily basis, as well as supplementary greens and fruits; the latter are welcomed by the smaller species also. Both groups love treats like millet spray and honey sticks.

Food for Parrots

The parrots are the last of the seedeaters to be considered. A common misconception is that parrots will do well on a diet of sunflower seeds and

Foods for large psittacines: Top (left to right): pellets, safflower, and beans; bottom (left to right): sunflower seed, peanuts, and corn. Vegetables and greens (middle) are an integral part of a balanced diet.

Heavy food and/or water containers are necessary for the larger hookbill species.

little else. Nothing can be further from the truth. Indeed, a parrot can live for many years with the most unsuitable food but the outcome is unfortunate. The bird may lose all of its feathers suddenly, and one morning you will find a naked bird sitting on its perch. Once this happens, it is almost impossible to put right. Do not be misled if your parrots pick out all of the sunflower seeds from the following mixture. When hungry, they'll eat the rest!

Sunflower seed	· 15%
(medium and large)	
Safflower seed	10%
Canary-grass seed	10%
White millet	10%
Shelled walnuts	10%
Shelled Brazil nuts	10%
Dry dog kibble	10%
Peanuts	10%
(shelled or in the shell)	
Cracked corn	5%
Oat groats	5%
Niger seed (thistle)	5%

Feeding

Do not offer even occasional extra treats (such as a sugar lump or a piece of biscuit) although it is cute to see a parrot holding a cookie and seeming to say "thank you for your kindness." Instead, give your parrot a piece of willow or an elder branch, a dog biscuit, or a honey stick, and enjoy the antics which the bird performs, especially when he attacks the object with his beak.

How to Get Your Bird to Eat a Formulated Diet

During the legally required quarantine period (30 days), newly imported birds are introduced to various medicated seeds and other seeds they are not familiar with, such as sunflower seeds. By the time the birds are ready to be sold, they have fairly well adjusted to the common commercial seed mixtures. They are, however, rarely introduced to crumbles and pellets, and therefore are reluctant to try them. Fanciers who want to convert their birds to crumbles and pellets should follow these suggestions:

• Day 1 thru Day 5   Mix 50% crumbles or pellets with 50% of the bird's usual diet. Sprinkle some crumbles or pellets on the aviary or cage floor as well.

• Day 6 thru 9   Each day remove more seeds and replace this amount with crumbles or pellets.

• Day 10   Offer only crumbles or pellets.

As not all pet birds that are housed together, preferably in a warm, draft-free environment, change their diet at the same time, each bird should be carefully observed. Birds that have not changed should be returned to their regular seed diet and, if possible, housed in a separate cage. After a few weeks, put them to the test again.

Food for Insect-eaters

There are not too many aviculturists (yet!) who keep birds that are exclusively insectivorous. The main reason for this is that such birds can make a real mess of their accommodations with their droppings, which are very thin and foul smelling. This means that a daily change of the cage-tray bedding is a must.

Also, it is not always possible to obtain suitable food for such birds. Although there are good diets available commercially for insect-eaters, you should not make these a staple diet for your birds. Depending on their size, most insectivorous birds are fond of small or cut-up mealworms, fly maggots, cut-up earthworms, grasshoppers, small beetles, spiders, earwigs, and green flies. In other words, all insects we can find that are not too big.

We can ensure a continuous supply of small mealworms by breeding them ourselves; buying them can be an extremely expensive affair.

Mealworms

These are the larvae of certain beetles; they should be available throughout the year, particularly during the breeding season. To breed them, first collect a few beetles. In a box of about $20 \times 10 \times 10$ inches ($50 \times 25 \times 25$ cm), drill three holes of approximately $1\frac{1}{4}$ inches (3 cm) diameter on each side. Cover the inside of these holes with gauze to prevent the beetles from getting out. The holes should be drilled at a height of $\frac{3}{4}$ inch (2 cm) away from the bottom. To avoid the rotting, line the box with plastic or sheet zinc, making sure that the holes are left free. Cover the box with a well-fitting lid, again to prevent the beetles from escaping and also to lessen the smell.

Above left: Cockatoos are intelligent and friendly birds that are willing to brood, usually during the spring.
Above right: The green-winged macaw or marron lives in hilly country and forest in small groups.
Below left: The scarlet macaw likes light woodland and savannah as habitat.
Below right: The blue and yellow macaw, from Panama to norther Paraguay, is still quite common in some areas!

48

Feeding

For better ventilation, drill a few holes in the lid as well. These can be a bit bigger than 1¼ inches (3 cm). Cover the inside of the holes with gauze and the rest of the lid with plastic or sheet zinc. Add a layer of straw. On top of the straw put a piece of old towel and cover this with 1½ inches (4 cm) of bran. On top of the bran put another piece of old towel and another layer of bran. Continue to about 1¼ inches (3 cm) from the top edge of the box. Cover it all with a cloth (which must not be too thick, so that the lid closes well) and finally a sheet of cardboard. On this piece of cardboard put soaked white bread, pieces of fruit, or greenstuff. Once a week you can gather the mealworms that are ready to eat from the cardboard. Wash them well and offer them to your birds. Don't forget that some birds must not have too many because they might get too fat and, as breeding birds, be of little or no value. You should cut off the heads of worms fed to young or small birds in your aviary. This is because mealworms swallowed alive can gnaw through a bird's crop with unpleasant results.

If you have a large number of insectivorous birds, it is best to prepare several cultures in separate boxes and use them in turn.

Maggots

Only a few bird fanciers are tempted to breed maggots. I must confess it is not a pleasant business. If you have a big garden, you can use a hidden spot to hang up a piece of meat or rotten fish. The flies will lay eggs on it. After a few days put the meat or the fish in a can that closes well. After another few days you will have as many maggots as you need.

Don't give these to the birds immediately. Rinse them first for at least 15 minutes under a weak spray of water. This takes care of the evacuation of the maggots' intestines. The maggots then become white and can be given to the birds. Less troublesome and less unpleasant is breeding maggots in preserve glasses. Fill a jar with boiled potatoes and sour milk and put it outside without a lid. After a few days close the jar. After a few more days the maggots will start developing.

Enchytraes or White Worms

You can find breeding pairs of these creatures beneath rotting wood and leaves. They are small, thin, white worms. You can easily breed them in a box 13 × 13 × 10 inches (35 × 35 × 25 cm). Fill the box with peat and good leafy earth. The whole thing must not be too firm but loose, and not too dry. With a spade make a hole about 6 inches (15 cm) diameter in the middle of the box. On the bottom put a slice of soaked white bread and the worms. Then cover the box with a glass lid and newspaper so that it remains dark inside. Check regularly to see that the bottom is not too dry and that enough food is available for the worms. After a few weeks you can harvest them. Rinse them and you have excellent food for your birds, especially during breeding time. Temperature for successful breeding is about 54°F (12°C).

Ant Pupae

You can also look for ant pupae. Whenever the sun shines on a summer day, the ants place their pupae in the upper part of the nest. Lay a white cloth near the nest and place a number of upturned plant pots around the edges, but leave a space under the edge of the pots where the ants can gain access. Now dig up the top part of the ant nest with a shovel and place it on the white cloth. The ants will busily rescue their pupae and carry them into the dark under the plant pots, from where you can easily collect them. These ant pupae can be dried and stored for use in the winter. The pupae are spread

Above left: The tiny African golden-breasted waxbill will breed in a well-planted aviary.
Above right: The red-billed fire finch, also known as the common or Senegal fire finch, is a good breeder.
Below left: The zebra finch, now available in many interesting color mutations, is very prolific.
Below right: The common waxbill or St. Helena waxbill has an excellent breeding record.

Feeding

out on paper or cardboard and allowed to dry out in the sun. When they are dry, they should be stored in a cool but damp-free spot. If allowed to get damp, ant pupae will decay quickly and become worthless. Before feeding to the birds in the winter, the pupae can be soaked for a few minutes in water. They will swell and can then be mixed with the regular insect food.

Other Insects

In the summer, other insect species can be collected in a net made from nylon gauze. The net is fastened to a long pole. Our method is to ride our bicycles along grassy banks while holding the mouth of the net in the long grass. At regular intervals we stop and empty the contents of the net into a container. It is possible to collect a great variety of grasshoppers, beetles, spiders, and so forth by using this method.

It is important to remember that all insect-eaters are also fruit-eaters (and are often collectively called soft-billed birds). Therefore fruit should not be absent from their diet. Further, many so-called seedeaters and various parrotlike birds will rear their young in the breeding season with insects as a supplement to their normal food. Small exotics will welcome mosquito larvae, waterfleas (*Daphnia*), and also tubifex, which can be obtained from aquarium suppliers. Moreover, these foods are excellent for canaries, flamingos, and other birds that possess the red factor gene (and, hence, red feathers), especially during the molt.

Food for Fruit-eaters

Like insect-eating birds, fruit-eaters pose problems when it comes to keeping their accommodations clean. Feeding fruit-eaters is somewhat easier than feeding insect-eaters—though the former will not refuse the odd mealworm. You can obtain commercially very good mixtures (called universal

food) for soft-billed birds which fulfill all requirements. They contain, among other things, berries, raisins, honey, dried insects, crawfish, vitamins, and minerals. But although this commercial food is easy to buy, it is also expensive! Therefore, in addition to the universal food, you can also give all sorts of fruit. What kind depends on the time of the year. But whatever kind of fruit is given, it must not be rotten; all rotten parts should be removed before the fruit is offered to the birds.

If we were to enumerate the advantages of various fruits, oranges and grapefruits would be the winners. These juicy fruits can be cut in thirds and placed in the cage or aviary, and the birds will peck out the contents. If you have newly imported birds, part of the orange may be hollowed out and filled with a mixture of universal food and the removed pulp. The new birds will quickly learn to recognize this soft food and will take it when no fruit is available.

The reason we cut an orange into thirds and not in half is because many fruit-eaters, for example the white-eyed zosterops, possess very fine beaks. These birds could penetrate deeply into the orange-pulp with their beaks and suffocate before they had time to withdraw. Halved apples and pears are also loved by the birds and they will soon peck them clean.

In order to prevent the fruit from being dragged all over the cage or aviary, one can use a plank with a number of nails hammered into it. A piece of orange, apple, or pear is then simply impaled on each nail. This prevents the fruit from becoming soiled.

It is also a good idea sometimes to cut the fruit very fine and mix it with the universal food. The juice of half an orange can also be mixed in and, if necessary, vitamin and mineral supplements.

Other fruits which can be given include: bananas (not too much, they are fattening), cherries, grapes, strawberries, currants, raisins, figs, dates, elderberries, plums, cotoneaster berries, gooseberries, grapefruit, guava, hawthorn, mulberries, papayas, peach, pineapple, pomegranate, pumpkin, raspberries, rose hip, tangerines, and tomato. Elderberries and plums can be hung in the aviary with leaves, twigs, and all so that the birds can obtain their food in a more natural manner.

When cherries or grapes are given, it is best to first remove the pits or seeds to avoid the possibility of any bird choking on them.

Any above-named fruits can be given not only to fruit-eaters. Many birds are keen on the occasional bit of fruit but will not consume as much of it as the fruit-eaters. But go easy on the fruit with canaries and diverse tropical birds, as well as parrotlike birds. A small piece of apple, pear, or orange is adequate.

Green Food

You already know that birds cannot be kept in top condition on a diet of seed only and that you should give them an occasional piece of fruit. Green food is another essential food item.

In the breeding season especially, there are many birds, in particular the canary and various tropical finches, that feed their young with green food. However, you must bear in mind that some bird species are rather particular as to what kind of green food they will eat. What one species will eat may be completely disregarded by another. By experimenting, you will find out what your birds prefer. But do no give them their favorite foods all the time; let them eat other things as well—it is for their own good.

In general we can say that all birds love lettuce. Caution is advised, as fresh lettuce can be dangerous, while polluted lettuce can be fatal. It is best to rinse the lettuce under a running tap and then to dry it with a clean cloth. If the lettuce is not used up in one day, you can easily keep it by cutting a piece from the base of the stem and placing it in water in a cool place. In addition to lettuce, endives are also

good, but you must take the same precautions.

Other green foods that may be enjoyed by your birds include curly kale, parsley, brussels sprouts, spinach, celery, chicory, cabbage heart, cucumber, sweet potato, beet, hydroponic-sprouted oats or barley, tomato, turnip greens, fresh corn (especially if it is at the "milky" stage; parrotlike birds love it!), acacia blossoms, alfalfa, calendula buds, dock, lantana blossoms, Swiss chard, watercress, and zucchini.

Although not a green, carrots are a very good vegetable food. You can hang a carrot to a nail like an apple, but it is better grated and mixed with egg or rearing food. It will be taken eagerly. For fruit-eating birds, the grated carrot can be mixed with universal food. Carrots have the advantage of providing the birds with carotene, which is converted to vitamin A in the liver. Birds that have the red factor, hence red feathers, should not go without this carotene if their plumage is to remain in good color. Be careful not to overfeed with carrots; too much can cause liver complaints. Other green foods with ample carotene include spinach, the tops of young nettles, and sweet peppers. All these are greedily eaten by birds. Thistle seeds also contain carotene.

Wild plants that can be fed include dandelion (both plant and roots!), hearts of shepherd's purse, sow thistle, and chickweed. The latter may be found in your own garden. Whenever you do a bit of weeding you can keep your birds in green food all summer long.

Egg Food or Rearing Food

Most breeders with many years of experience make their own egg foods and usually have very good results. But experiments have shown that many of these feeds are made much too rich. We are dealing with a very small bird and to stuff it with fats, carbohydrates, vitamins, and whatever else is

Feeding

Average Composition of Some Commonly Used Vegetables for Pet Birds

Per 100 g consumed food	Protein (g)	Fat (g)	Carbohydrates (g)	Na (mg)	K (mg)	Ca (mg)	P (mg)	Fe (IU)	Vitamin A (IU)	Vitamin B$_1$ (mg)	Vitamin B$_2$ (mg)	Vitamin C (mg)
Carrot	1.0	0.2	7.3	45	280	35	30	0.7	13,500	70	55	6
Corn salad	1.8	0.4	2.6	4	420	30	50	2.0	7,000	65	80	30
Endive	1.7	0.2	2.0	50	350	50	50	1.4	900	52	120	9
Lettuce	1.2	0.2	1.7	8	220	20	35	0.6	1,500	60	90	10
Parsley	4.4	0.4	9.8	30	1000	240	130	8.0	12,080	140	300	170
Radish	1.0	0.1	3.5	17	255	34	26	1.5	38	33	30	30
Red beet	1.5	0.1	7.6	86	340	30	45	0.9	80	22	40	10
Spinach	2.4	0.4	2.4	60	660	110	48	3.0	8,200	86	240	47

not the proper way to feed it; the opposite of what is required will be achieved. More young birds in the nest are lost from overfeeding than from the cold.

Should commercial egg food be used exclusively, buy only from reputable companies and preferably use only those products that list the contents clearly on the package.

Basically an egg food is required that contains the correct types and amounts of vitamins. Unfortunately, many vitamin preparations come in such large quantities that the effectiveness of these micronutrients is lost before the preparation can all be used. Fortunately, it is possible to put together a good, nutritionally balanced food without making it too rich. The following steps may be taken: Beat a chicken's egg and make an omelette with a little butter or margarine. After it is cooled, the omelette is mashed up with a fork and mixed with the crumbs of four rusks. To this is added one-quarter of a grated apple or pear and the juice of half an orange, and all is mixed well together. This soft food is greedily taken by all birds and they feed their young with it. It is also a good idea once or twice a week to take a slice of stale white or brown bread and soak it in water. Then squeeze out all the excess moisture and pour a little milk or skimmed milk over it. Birds love this mixture and tropical birds in particular will feed it eagerly to their young.

First thing every morning before feeding, each hand-reared parrot or parakeet chick should be accurately weighed on a gram scale and the weight recorded on a special chart.

Feeding

Cod-liver oil may be added but extremely sparingly, as excessive amounts can be more dangerous than we realize.

Fat

During the winter birds require animal fat. This applies especially to aviary birds, which are exposed to the frequent weather changes in our colder states. During the months containing the letter "r", you can hang up a piece of suet near a perch. Commercially prepared "seed-bells" for wild birds can also be used.

Vitamins

Very often, perhaps too often, you hear aviculturists and avian veterinarians discuss the importance of vitamins. Although life itself is not possible without vitamins, there is not much point in discussing their pros and cons when you have little idea as to what vitamins are. We have all seen breeder's premises that contain a veritable arsenal of vitamin preparations on the windowsill, almost resembling a dispensary. Vitamins are useful, but they must be used with caution, as too great a dose can be positively dangerous to birds. Moreover, they should not be stored on the windowsill as strong light will affect them and render them useless. Cod-liver oil, for example, loses its potency in strong light and also goes rancid. Preparations should not be kept for too long; buy them from a reliable dealer who has not stored them too long. They are best kept in a cool, dark room, for example, the cellar.

In brief, here are some key reasons why vitamins are essential to the pet-bird diet.

• Vitamin A is essential for growth, sound skin and feathers, food fertilization, and prevention of night blindness. Good sources are cod-liver oil, corn, wheat germ, green feed, milk, and carrots.

• The Vitamin-B complex includes some 14 vitamins, most of which can be found in yeast. That is why I often recommend feeding whole-wheat bread to cage and aviary birds, preferably soaked in milk. (Be careful it doesn't turn sour.) Other good sources are cod-liver oil, milk, green feed, and sprouted seed. The B vitamins promote digestion of carbohydrates, promote growth, and prevent anemia.

• Birds can produce vitamin C in their bodies. However, it is found in various vegetables, oranges, and lemons. Vitamin C promotes resistance to disease and aids in the healing of wounds. Research has shown, however, that the red-eared bulbul cannot synthesize vitamin C, and therefore it must be provided in the feed.

• Birds can also produce vitamin D if they have access to ultraviolet light. However, they can utilize only vitamin D_3; vitamin D_2 cannot be converted into D_3 in their bodies. Good sources of vitamin D are cod-liver oil and milk. Vitamin D is essential for the normal development of bone structure.

• Vitamin E promotes fertility and is found in sprouted seed, especially wheat seed.

• Vitamin K, from the Danish *koagulation* (coagulation) is essential for the proper functioning of the liver and for blood clotting. Good sources are green-plant parts, liver, roots, soybeans, and various grains. The bird diet requires only extremely small quantities, and a good menu will satisfy their needs adequately. There is no real need to furnish a vitamin K supplement.

Take note: Be sparing with vitamins; quantities in your birds' food should already be more than is necessary. The use of vitamins A and D or cod-liver oil in the months with an "r" is not wrong, but use no more than ½ teaspoon of cod-liver oil to 2 pounds (.9 kg) of food, or 4 to 5 drops of vitamins A and D to 2 pounds (.9 kg) of seed. Unlike the water-soluble vitamins, both A and D are stored in the body. Excessive amounts can accumulate and may actually have harmful effects.

Feeding

Calcium

Although calcium is not required by birds for the entire year, it is recommended that it be made available at all times. The best method of supplying this mineral is with cuttlefish bones, which can be placed here and there near perches. Alternatively, a bowl of grit (see page 57) and dicalcium phosphate can be placed in the aviary. Cage birds can be given a piece of cuttlefish bone between the wires or in a holder. Birds need calcium especially during the breeding season when the eggs are being formed, and during the molt. Calcium is necessary for proper functioning of the heart, muscles, blood, and nervous system.

Drinking Water

Although water is not a food, I will deal with it here. In the first place, you must ensure that your

Cuttlefish bone is an excellent calcium supplement. It must be uncontaminated by oil, and thoroughly cleaned,

birds have fresh water available at all times, and that the water cannot become polluted. In the aviary, it is best to place the water container on a slab. There are two reasons for this: first, the water is more likely to stay cool in the summer, especially if we are talking about earthenware containers; second, the vessel is less likely to collect dirt than if it were placed simply on the ground. In cages, take care never to place drinking or feeding dishes below the perches.

A very good drink to give your birds once a week is honey water. This is made simply by dissolving 1 tablespoon of honey in about 5 tablespoons of warm water. After cooling, pour it in the water dish and give it to the birds. Another honey drink, which is even more nutritious, can be prepared as follows: 1 tablespoon of honey, 1 tablespoon of condensed milk (unsweetened), and, optionally, 1 tablespoon of baby food consisting of mixed vegetables and meat. This is all mixed together in 10 tablespoons of warm water.

In winter, providing water in an unheated outside aviary can pose some problems, especially when it begins to freeze. Many bird keepers warm the water with little oil lamps or candles. I cannot recommend this practice. We are not really helping when the birds drink water that is too warm. They may also warm themselves at the lamps, possibly with dangerous consequences. Serious burns have been known to result from this well-meaning but ill-advised practice.

The best method is to give sugar water to the birds in the winter (1 tablespoon of sugar in about 10 tablespoons of water) but make sure that they cannot bathe in it. Sugar water has the advantage of not freezing so quickly and, even when it does, it freezes in a soft mass rather than as hard ice. The above-mentioned honey drink may also be used since it has similar properties.

Bath water should also remain clean at all times. Thus clean bath and drinking water should be given daily. On warm summer days, change the bath water twice a day if possible.

Feeding

Grit

Many veterinarians and some aviculturists tend to disagree on the necessity of a daily supply of grit. This does not mean, however, that seed-eating birds both in the wild and in the aviary are not dependent upon small gravel and grit that they pick up from the soil, so that their alimentary system works efficiently in the digestion of seeds. Seed-eating birds have a crop in which the seed is softened before it goes into the gizzard or muscular stomach (the gizzard is an enlargement of the alimentary canal with dense, muscular walls). Without gravel or grit (often ground-up *white* oyster shell, as gray or dark shells are believed to contain too much lead), a great deal of the seed remains unground and whole seeds are passed out in the droppings.

Experiments have shown that birds that have no access to grit take greater quantities of food than those that have a supply of grit. Moreover, the health of the bird declines. The undigested seeds cause blockages in the intestines and then the only discharge is a whitish, watery substance.

In various commercial brands of grit, redstone, chalk, gravel, and calcareous seaweed (or kelp), as well as a little charcoal, are added. In the wild, various birds take little bits of charcoal before going to nest; but the necessity of a daily supply of charcoal is questionable as it is suspected of absorbing vitamins A, B_2, and K from the intestinal tract. If this is correct, it can mean that charcoal can cause vitamin-deficiency diseases. Grit also frequently contains crushed quartz, which is a very hard substance, is insoluble, and has sharp edges which give an even better grinding effect in the gizzard.

Never use grit as the sole source of certain essential minerals which may be contained in it, for example calcium, iron, magnesium, and iodine. In other words, offer a variety of food to ensure that sufficient quantities of minerals are available. An overdose of mineralized grit can cause damage to the kidneys. Most aviculturists supply a separate dish with grit once or twice a month (especially for the larger birds, like parrots). Some maintain that grit on the floor of a cage or indoor aviary helps to keep the feet of small birds clean. The fact that the birds make regular use of the grit can have only good consequences.

Grit is available in various grades: fine or small for finches, canaries, parakeets and similar-sized bird species; and medium to coarse for large parrots and parakeets.

Diseases, Accidents, and Injuries

This chapter will deal with medicating your pet birds. This is, at best, a tricky topic and I do not intend to promote any remedies or unnecessary treatments. I believe in conservative treatment and I put my primary emphasis on prevention and the recognition of symptoms for you to describe to your *avian* veterinarian.

In the course of a long career, I have dealt with many types of birds. I have cared for them, arranged their breeding, studied them, and admired them. I have also done all I could to promote their well-being. Even so, I have had birds get sick in my cages and aviaries; they have even died. This is not so surprising—why should the situation in captivity be different from that in nature? Illness and death are the ever-present companions of everything that lives and grows.

When I was a student biologist, I once determined that the annual rate of mortality for the larger birds in their native habitat varies between 30% and 40%; the annual mortality of small songbirds varies between 40% and 60%. Those are tremendously high percentages. They mean that most songbirds in nature don't live beyond 1½ to 2½ years of age.

In comparison with these percentages, the situation among pet birds seems quite favorable. The average age at death of all pet birds is much higher, and lovebirds, budgerigars, and canaries of 10 to 15 and more years of age are not a rarity (see page 14). You can aspire to this level of success if you are willing to care for your stock as well as possible. If you call yourself a bird fancier, you will surely want to lower the death rate of your birds as much as possible. This means that you will try to heal your sick birds with all the methods at your command, even if you notice rather quickly that you have started a difficult task that as often as not provides little satisfaction. Treating the illness of birds is difficult. A correct diagnosis is even more difficult to make and often you have to treat birds even if you are in the dark as to precisely what is wrong with them.

For that reason I keep emphasizing that prevent-

The correct way to hold a small bird.

ing illnesses of pet birds is very important. Unfortunately, even the best care cannot prevent all illness. Healthy birds can catch cold or become afflicted with parasites or infected with viruses or germs. In short, birds, like all living things, are subject to the laws of sickness and health, life and death.

As a bird fancier, it is important to know what a healthy bird looks like. In case of any deviations,

The correct way to hold a medium–sized bird (see also the drawing on page 41).

58

you can then promptly note it and take action. Experience is important in this respect. You can be a born bird lover, but you still need years of experience to be a bird expert. And even a bird expert doesn't hesitate to ask help and advice from an avian veterinarian. If no one with that specialty is available in your immediate area, write to the Association of Avian Veterinarians, P.O. Box 299, East Northport, NY 11731 or telephone (516) 757-6320. They should be able to put you in touch with a veterinarian who works with birds.

The experienced bird fancier can see at a glance if something is wrong with his birds. That's a real advantage, as the inexperienced hobbyist tends to become aware of problems more slowly and often it is then too late to help the birds. That is why it is of the utmost importance to check on the birds every day—and with a careful eye. Don't skip a single bird. Become aware of any change in their looks or activities and be ready to respond quickly.

The Sick Bird

A bird in a cage or aviary is much better off than it would be free in nature; it is protected from bad weather conditions and predators, and is provided with all that it can desire. But as soon as a bird falls sick, it loses its bloom, its song, its activity, and its keen look. Its feathers will fluff out, it will sit hunched up in some corner and sleep a lot, it loses much of its alertness and, frequently, may spend more time than usual at the feed dish. It also will lose interest in its surroundings, and will lose weight and the gloss in its plumage; its eyes will appear dull and lifeless. The experienced bird keeper will be able to recognize signs of sickness in his birds at a glance. This fact means—as stated before—that the experienced hobbyist has a certain advantage over the newcomer, who may not recognize the danger signs until it is too late to do anything about it.

It is therefore essential that bird keepers examine their birds daily, so that they will soon learn to recognize what is normal and what is unnatural behavior, which could point to the beginnings of a disease outbreak. No single bird should be overlooked in these daily observations. The birds' droppings should also be examined for signs of abnormality. Those of seed-eating birds should be reasonably firm. Thin, watery, colorless, or unusually colored droppings can indicate enteric diseases (infections of the bowel) or can be a symptom of other ailments.

With soft-billed birds, the droppings are naturally thin and it takes experience to recognize signs of bad health. Whenever any bird shows the slightest signs of sickness, it is imperative that *immediate* action be taken.

Never wait for the symptoms to become worse or more apparent, and never think: "This has come by itself, and will go away by itself." Diseases do not come by themselves and they certainly will not go away by themselves. Should one fail to take immediate action, the possibility arises that the disease will get such a grip that even the best treatment will be to no avail. Then what do you do with a bird showing symptoms of sickness?

Naturally, the first task will be to try to find out what type of disease you are dealing with, by a careful and systematic examination of the bird. In other words, try to make a diagnosis. This is not always easy. The bird fancier is not an avian veterinarian, and therefore not necessarily qualified to identify bird diseases at first sight. Even an expert can have problems with this task. Frequently an accurate and expert examination is required before one can tell what malady is affecting the bird.

Sometimes the symptoms give a clear indication, especially when they apply to those diseases with which the fancier has had experience in the past. Occasionally one may chance upon symptoms recognizable from the description of a certain sickness and be able to recognize the disease by looking for further signs. But one may often be groping in

Diseases, Accidents, and Injuries

Knowing a bird's anatomy and the various parts of its plumage is useful not only for conversations with veterinarians, but also for describing different bird species. The parts of a bird (in this case a long-tailed finch or *Poephila acuticauda*) are:

1. Crown	2. Forehead	3. Upper mandible	4. Lower mandible
5. Chin and throat	6. Breast	7. Front toes	8. Hind toe
9. Tibia	10. Cloaca and undertail feathers	11. Outer tail feathers	12. Uppertail coverts
13. Rump	14. Bend of wing	15. Back	16. Nape

the dark and may have to leave it to luck to find a cure for the sick bird.

In every case it is certainly worth the trouble to try every means possible to cure the bird. Even the cheapest birds have a right to live, and any fancier who does not do all he can to keep his birds living and healthy would be better off collecting stamps! One learns by practice and if you take the necessary

Diseases, Accidents, and Injuries

precautions in the use of medications, you will not make too many mistakes. On the contrary, every time a bird is saved from otherwise certain death, you will experience a great sense of satisfaction and accomplishment.

Carefully remove the sick bird from the cage or aviary and subject it to the minutest examination. Blow on the feathers around the vent. If the surrounding area is wet and sticky, this points to the possibility of a nutritional disturbance or a bacterial

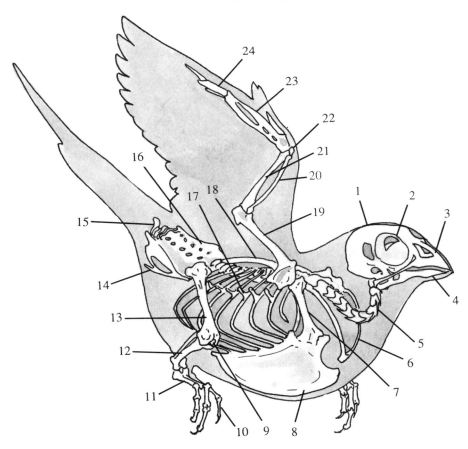

Skeleton of a long–tailed finch (*Poephila acuticauda*).

1. Skull	2. Foramen	3. Upper mandible	4. Lower mandible	5. Vertebrae column	6. Clavicle
7. Coracoid	8. Sternum	9. Patella	10. Phalanges	11. Tarsus	12. Tibia and fibula
13. Femur	14. Pelvis	15. Pygostyle	16. Ischium	17. Ribs	18. Scapula
19. Humerus	20. Radius	21. Ulna	22. Carpals	23. Metacarpus	24. Phalanges

Diseases, Accidents, and Injuries

infection of the gut. In many such cases, the flesh around the vent will appear red and inflamed. Feel the bird's breast carefully on either side of the sternum. If it feels sharp, and if the flesh on either side of the sternum is lean and limp, this is always an indication that the bird's health leaves much to be desired. Damp nostrils and a wheezing breath are a sign of respiratory infection, and an open beak could indicate aspergillosis or pox. In the latter case, this notorious disease (see page 70) is to be seen mainly around the eyes and on the feet. In particular, look carefully at the eyes, which may have inflamed lids. Feel the feet and the wings gently for signs of fractures; look under the wings; blow the feathers aside and examine carefully—if necessary with a magnifying glass—for signs of parasites. Examine the entire body for wounds or abscesses. If the bird is a female, gently palpate the

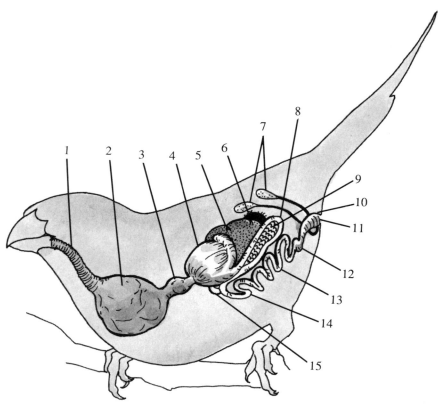

Some internal organs:

1. Esophagus	2. Crop	3. Proventriculus	4. Ventriculus or gizzard	5. Liver
6. Spleen	7. Kidneys	8. Duodenum	9. Pancreas	10. Cloaca
11. Anus or vent	12. Caecum	13. Ileum (small intestine)	14. Jejunum	15. Gall

Diseases, Accidents, and Injuries

lower abdomen for signs of egg binding.

With no obvious diagnosis, ask yourself the following questions: Is the bird receiving a balanced diet? Or is it suffering from a deficiency of protein, or vitamins, or calcium? Was the drinking water so foul that the bird has become sick from drinking it? Has the bird been sitting in a draft or has there been a sudden change in the temperature? Could it be a possibility of poisoning through the food? In short, investigate every possible cause, and try to discover every symptom. Once you are on the right track, it will be much easier for you to find the right cure.

After the examination, the bird should be placed in a warm place, preferably in a hospital cage. Should a hospital cage not be available, then a small cage will do. The cage should be covered with a cloth, but leave a small opening at the front. The bird can then sit quietly and, as the sun shines, the cage can be turned so that the sunlight almost shines into it. Extra warmth, provided by an electric light,

A sick diamond finch on the bottom of the cage. Note the fluffed out feathers and the hunched over body.

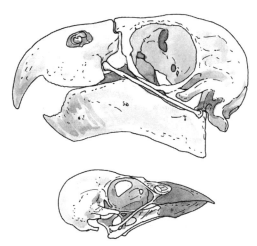

The skull of an Amazon parrot and a common sparrow (not in proportion to each other). In addition to light feathers and a light skeleton, all modern bird species also possess a light skull, as their teeth have been eliminated.

is also recommended. While the bird is in the sick cage, it can be further observed for symptoms not discovered in the initial examination. You can view the situation more closely, while being reassured that the sick bird cannot infect its companions in the aviary.

The Hospital Cage

Many types of hospital cages are available from avicultural suppliers. The size of the cage you acquire will, of course, be decided by the type of birds you keep. The hospital cage should be placed in a room that is seldom used, where no other birds are kept, and that can be well ventilated without any unpleasant drafts.

At the outset, the temperature in the hospital cage should be maintained at 85° to 90°F (29°–33°C). A thermometer should be placed in the cage, but not where it can be reached by the bird;

parakeets, or parrots in particular, will make short work of such an instrument. Should the temperature run too high, then one of the lamps may be turned off; or the temperature may be lowered by increasing the ventilation. There are openings in the lower part of the hospital cage through which cold air enters, is heated by lamps, and then rises by convection into the main cage area. Remember that a sick bird requires fresh air and be sure that there is always a vent open both at the bottom and the upper part of the cage.

The sick bird should be provided with its normal food, in the hope that it will continue to feed. Do not forget to offer it its favorite tidbits—you do not want it to become further weakened. Should the bird start to feed normally again, then it is often unnecessary to administer medicine. Given warmth and quiet, it will often effect a rapid recovery. As the bird improves, the temperature can be slowly reduced from day to day. This can be accomplished by switching off one lamp at a time, until soon the bird can be returned to its normal environment.

Take note of the following points:

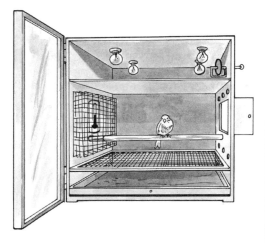

Hospital cage.

• Do not hesitate to consult an avian veterinarian should your sick bird fail to respond positively to hospital-cage treatment within 24 hours.
• Although this may sound pedantic, always take care of the healthy birds first each day before dealing with the patient, thus avoiding contamination (through the hands or through clothes).
• After each time the patient is handled, the hands should be thoroughly washed. Food and water containers also must be cleaned and disinfected several times daily.
• After the bird is cured, the hospital cage and all accessories should be thoroughly cleaned and disinfected.
• If you take a sick bird to a veterinarian, whenever possible, do so in its own cage. A bird that comes from an aviary is best carried in a cardboard carton (but be sure there are sufficient ventilation holes for breathing) or in a small rectangular cage.
• Try to take a feces (droppings) sample of the sick bird to the vet, and also let the vet examine the food which the bird normally eats. If you use paper on the floor of the cage, replace it a couple of hours before you take the bird to the vet, so that he has fresh samples to examine.
• Before carrying the cage to the car, pack it well in paper and cover it with a blanket, to prevent the possibility of chills. On cold days, such rules are obvious. On very cold days, it is advisable to warm up the car for a few minutes by running the engine before the cage is put inside. Birds can lose heat rapidly inside a car that has been standing in the cold for many hours.
• Use pet-shop medicines only when your avian veterinarian has suggested them. Remember that avian medicines are constantly being re-evaluated and upgraded. Sick birds should have the best available drugs administered in the correct dosage. The administration of "medicines-for-all-ailments" may interfere with the veterinarian's treatment. Avoid using human medicines unless recommended by the veterinarian. (Kaopectate, for instance, is be a good treatment for loose droppings.)

Diseases, Accidents, and Injuries

Causes for Concern

When nearly all of your birds become sick and start to die prompt action is essential. Sometimes an outbreak of disease can be a real calamity for the fancier. There are diseases which, in a short time, can decimate an aviary full of birds.

Canary fanciers know well the dreaded canary pox; budgerigar keepers fear psittacosis; pheasant and quail breeders the "blackhead." Newcastle disease, Pacheco's disease, or French molt, can all soon destroy the pleasure that one has with pet birds.

Should you be unfortunate enough to have an epidemic break out among your stock, there are a few immediate basic measures to take. All sick birds and those showing the slightest symptoms should be isolated. All other birds should be placed separately in another aviary or other cages and the original aviary should be thoroughly cleaned out and disinfected. If you do not know what disease is affecting your stock, you must enlist the help of an avian veterinarian as soon as possible. He will undoubtedly want to examine any dead birds as soon as possible. With an outbreak of serious disease, birds showing symptoms must immediately be separated. There may still be a chance of saving a few birds. Leave the healthy birds in a roomy cage, and treat all cages that have been in contact with the sick birds with one of the following products:
• *Lysol*: Dilution—4 ounces per gallon of water. An excellent all-purpose disinfectant.
• *One-Stroke-Environ* (the official disinfectant of the United States Department of Agriculture): Dilution—½ ounce per gallon of water.
• *Clorox*: Dilution—6 ounces per gallon of water. May be corrosive to bare metal; excellent for concrete flooring.

Treated cages should not be used again until they are thoroughly dry. Now for the question: What do we do with a bird when it is no longer possible to save it? Whether a sick bird should be quickly put out of its misery, or whether nature should be allowed to take its own course is a question often discussed by fanciers. Many aviculturists are unable to make a decision themselves as they are unable to imagine how much a bird may suffer, or how much pain it may feel. The best policy in such cases is to take the sick bird to an avian veterinarian, who will quickly and painlessly euthanize the patient.

The First Treatment

As we have already noted, the first treatment for a sick bird should be carried out immediately after symptoms have been recognized. The bird is placed in a hospital cage or in a warm, draft-free spot, so that warmth and quiet help to increase the chances of a cure. At this stage it is not essential to begin treating with drugs or medicine. First, aided by peace and warmth, allow nature the possibility of curing the disease. If, after 24 hours, you see that the bird has been feeding and has begun to lose its sick appearance, then in almost every case a full recov-

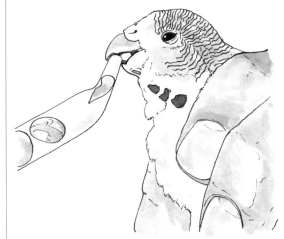

Oral medication can be administered by using a small plastic medicine dropper.

Diseases, Accidents, and Injuries

ery is mostly just a matter of a few days.

Should the bird really show no signs of improvement, then you can begin with a plastic medicine dropper (which can be obtained for a few cents from any drugstore) to administer a few drops of glucose via the beak. Should the bird then want to eat, you can try feeding it some stale bread soaked in milk, some canary-rearing or egg food, oatmeal porridge, or soft bird pellets, as a weakened bird will be unable to shell its seed. If the bird then begins to eat well, you can assume that you have won the first stage of the battle.

One mistake frequently made in the administration of medicines to birds is to overdose. People who may be extremely cautious themselves when taking medicines prescribed by the doctor, may approach their sick birds with the idea that "the first blow is half the battle." The result is that the bird is given far too much medicine, or too strong a solution. A person weighing 170 lbs (77kg) may take one or two aspirins (*not* a medicine for birds), but even a tenth part of an aspirin would be a massive overdose for a bird weighing barely half an ounce. Therefore, always administer medicine to birds with the greatest caution. I have mentioned aspirin as an example, as many bird fanciers (and other animal lovers) are convinced that this is a wonder drug that can cure all manner of ailments. This is definitely a misconception. Be careful with medicines; follow the instructions of your veterinarian with the greatest care and never try to play the role of doctor. Never give medicines at random, as you do not know what their effect will be. The chance that you will give the correct dose is—if you are not a veterinarian—almost nil, but the chance that you will only make the bird sicker is very possible.

In many cases, it is necessary to administer medicine to a bird directly in the beak. This may be done with a plastic dropper (glass is likely to break). A few drops of the medicine are sucked up in the dropper and the bird is taken in the left hand. The beak is gently opened with a pointed matchstick and the medicine is dropped into the cavity of the throat.

It is dangerous to push the nozzle of the dropper into the throat cavity as medicine may find its way into the lungs or the air sacs. (See page 58 for drawings showing the proper way to hold birds while administering medication.)

Abscesses: Budgerigars (parakeets) are especially prone to abscesses, usually above the eyes, along the roof of the mouth, below the tongue (white spots), and on the underside of the feet (bumble-feet). An abscess is a localized collection of white, cheeselike, and crumbly material (pus), formed by tissue disintegration and surrounded by an inflamed area. Most abscesses can be treated with antibiotics. Obtain the advice of your avian veterinarian on what type to use.

Aspergillosis: This condition is caused by the inhalation of the spore of the fungus *Aspergillosis fumigatus*. It mainly affects the larger parrots and parakeets and can be very troublesome; budgies, lovebirds, and passerines (finches) are less often plagued with the condition. Unfortunately, the symptoms are difficult to recognize. Usually, the patient shows some difficulty in breathing and there can be a discharge from the nostrils. Add 2½ grains of potassium iodine to every 2 fluid ounces of water (60 ml) as a preventive measure. To date, no satisfactory treatment for this disease has been discovered and accurate diagnosis usually only follows a postmortem examination.

Asthma: To date, I have come across this condition only in budgerigars and other parrotlike birds, and fortunately, it occurs only sporadically.

Above left: Thanks to the red or hooded siskin, the red factor was brought into the canary.
Above right: The red-cheeked cordon bleu is generally a good breeder but requires live food throughout the year.
Below left: The white-headed nun is a shy bird from southern Thailand, Malaysia, Sumatra, Java, and Bali.
Below right: Society finches or Bengalese are free, hardy breeders and excellent foster parents.

Diseases, Accidents, and Injuries

The cause is not yet fully understood but it is probably brought on by an infection of the lungs or air sacs, the inhalation of dust, poisonous fumes, pollen, etc. The illness is easy to recognize by labored breathing and a wide-open beak. Sometimes a squeaking noise can be heard as the bird inhales. The bird sits uncomfortably on its perch and tries hard to keep its balance. The feathers are usually ruffled. Sometimes it can happen that the bird is normally in the best of health and then suddenly gets an asthma attack at different times of the day. A satisfactory remedy has not yet been found but the condition should be referred to a veterinarian. Ensure that the room in which the cage is kept is well ventilated, but beware of drafts.

Bald Spots: Parrots, parakeets and other pet birds are seldom infested with external parasites, but infestation can happen, particularly with red mites. I know of cases started by sparrows dropping their feathers while roosting on the roof of an aviary. Newly imported lovebirds can also suffer from a range of parasites; you will be able to spot them by their "moth-eaten" feathers and bald spots.

The large red mite (about 1 millimeter long) survives on blood that it sucks from birds. Its life cycle generally doesn't exceed three weeks. In that time, it lays its eggs in crevices and cracks. In a warm and somewhat humid environment, these eggs hatch in 48 to 72 hours, spend several days as larvae, and then develop into adults.

Mites attack birds of all ages. Some mites specialize in certain bird species; some even attack humans. The red mite characteristically is active

only at night, and it is then that it bothers the birds. During the day the mites withdraw into their crevices and cracks. You can also find them under and behind cages, as well as in and behind nest boxes and other hiding places.

Because mites are active at night, infected nest boxes can cause birds a lot of discomfort. They don't give the birds a moment of rest as they suck their fill of blood. Before their meal, the mites are gray; afterwards they assume their typical red coloration. Infested birds frequently don't sleep at all during the night, and therefore sleep a lot during the day. Brooding birds can't stand staying on the nest if they suffer from mites, and infested young tend to leave the nest earlier than normal, often in a weak and poorly feathered condition.

Mites tend to multiply twice as fast during warm, humid weather. Large hordes can attack your sleeping birds, resulting in anemia, weakness, and even death. If you are trying to breed birds in infested aviaries, you may just as well give up. The mites may multiply to such an extent that you can stick a knife in any crack in the wood and come up with a blood-stained blade.

Many insecticides are effective against the red mite. Most of them contain pyrethrin, made from the pyrethrin flower grown in Kenya. Pyrethrin is harmless to birds and it is usually mixed with other equally harmless materials that activate pyrethrin, so that it does its job better.

With a parasite infestation, you can't take half measures. Put your birds in a temporary cage or aviary, as far away from the infested area as possible. Treat all nest boxes and sleeping cages with boiling water, using a small brush. Brush insecticide powder into all crevices, joints, cracks, and openings and clean off all perches and other furniture. Then rinse them with boiling water. Repeat this procedure after about five days and again after another week. Meanwhile, treat your birds with pyrethrin (or carbaryl), with special attention to the neck, the area around the vent, and under the wings. Don't put them back into their old quarters until

Above left: The Napoleon weaver is a hardy bird that needs germinated seeds and small insects.
Above right: The fire-crowned weaver or bishop is not suitable for a small cage or any indoor compartment.
Below left: The Gouldian finch is a very popular pet bird with many color mutations (e.g. a white-breasted form).
Below right: The cut-throat finch is often a free breeder, but also uses boxes or baskets.

Diseases, Accidents, and Injuries

everything there is completely dry.

To tell if you've been invaded by red mites, look for these signs of infestation: weaknesses and listlessness in otherwise healthy birds; constant searching with beaks through the feathers; restlessness at night; interruption of breeding; or neglect of the young.

Confirm your suspicions of red-mite infestation by catching one of your birds late in the evening and examining it under a strong light. If there is an infestation, you will be able to see the red mites run among the feathers and over your hand.

If you keep birds in a small cage, hang a white cloth over the cage at night. If you have red mites, you will be able to see them on the cloth the next morning. You can get rid of a good part of the infestation by putting the cloth in boiling water to kill the mites.

As I mentioned, parrots and parakeets seldom become infested with other types of parasites, such as lice, fleas, or ticks, all of which can be seen with the naked eye. Wild-caught and imported birds, however, often have ticks.

Ticks are gray and, like mites, belong to the arachnids. Ticks tend to let themselves drop off as soon as they have sucked their fill of blood. Once they digest their meal, they look for a new host. Don't worry if you can't tell a tick from a louse or flea. All three can be combatted with pyrethrin or carbaryl.

Repeat the treatment after several days to be sure you eliminate developing life stages—the young adults, the larvae, and the eggs (which can be seen as tiny white clusters, called "nits").

Burns: Burns caused by acids can best be treated with a thin coat of baking soda mixed half and half with water; alkali burns with vinegar; and heat burns (from oven, boiling water, burner, toaster) with an anti-inflammatory powder or spray (*not*, however, with butter, salad oils, grease, or first-aid ointments). In serious cases see your veterinarian, who may prescribe antibiotics.

Cancer: Unfortunately, pet birds are also sus-

ceptible to various types of cancer. It is obvious that an avian veterinarian should be consulted if cancer is suspected. There are internal forms—which are not immediately recognizable—and also external forms. Naturally, the symptoms vary, as cancer can affect different organs. The patient will quickly lose condition and sit miserably with ruffled feathers in some corner of the cage or aviary. The bird may often have its head tucked under its wing and may have difficulty walking (the feet and legs are usually swollen). In many cases diarrhea may develop, or even vomiting. There are some forms of cancer that can be removed by surgery, but in most cases it is best to put the patient out of its misery in a humane manner. It is best for this to be performed by a veterinarian.

Canary Pox: This disease is caused by a filterable virus. The virus is chiefly transmitted by biting insects, such as mosquitos. There are different kinds of viruses, specific to different groups of birds: chicken-pox virus, duck-pox virus, pigeon-pox virus, etc. The pox virus is especially difficult to destroy. Of the cage and aviary birds, canaries are particularly susceptible and they become very sick in a short time. Even parrots and parakeets (especially budgerigars and lovebirds) are not spared—there is psittacine-pox virus. The external symptoms include tiny skin swellings which are 1 to 3 millimeters in diameter and yellowish-white to yellowish-brown in color. These appear first on the eyelids, but later on the legs and feet, and finally on the entire skin. The incubation time for this skin virus is from 3 to 16 days. The first symptoms of infection are swollen, irritated eyelids. The patient will continuously scratch the eyelids with its feet and the infection will rapidly spread to the limbs. Now and again it happens that the pox blisters dry up and in 1 to 2 weeks gradually disappear, but more often the infection spreads to the mouth and respiratory organs, after which it usually becomes fatal. The patient becomes depressed, lets its wings hang under its body, and sits shivering with its feathers fluffed out; in most cases, diarrhea will also be

Diseases, Accidents, and Injuries

apparent. Death can follow in a few days. In dissecting the bird's body, one usually finds a lightly swollen spleen and an infection of the outer lungs. The diagnosis can be proven by taking a virus culture and doing a microscopic examination. Most attacks in canaries occur in youngsters 4 to 7 months old. The death rate from this disease can be as high as 90%!

The pox virus can be transmitted in the following ways:

• through saliva, nasal mucus, tears, and particles of skin from the infected canary;
• through biting insects, especially the mosquito;
• through the bird keeper, who may carry the virus on his shoes or clothing;
• through wild birds, especially sparrows and finches.

Vaccination is the only possible method of preventing this disease. Various commercially produced canary-pox vaccines are available; these are given in the wing web of the bird. After the vaccination, the weakened virus multiplies in the skin of the bird. The patient will show the usual wing hanging, but this is no cause for concern. After 7 to 10 days a pox blister may be seen at the sight of the vaccination, but this will disappear in 2 to 3 weeks. If no blister appears, we can come to one of the following conclusions:

• the bird was already immune to the disease;
• the vaccination graft has not taken;
• the vaccine has lost its properties and has therefore no effect.

Six weeks after the disappearance of this disease, the birds can be handled, entered in exhibitions, and so forth. It is recommended that an outbreak of any such disease be referred to an avian veterinarian.

In an infected aviary, it is possible—quite probable, in fact—that there are birds already infected with pox and others in which the disease is still in its incubation period; that is to say, already infected but with no symptoms. The following measures must be taken:

• Isolate *all* birds from the infected cage/aviary and have the veterinrian give them a canary-pox vaccination and 250 mg tetracycline (or chloramphenicol). Also, 5,000 units of vitamin A per $3^1/_2$ ounces (100 ml) should be added to the drinking water. There is a good chance that the vaccination, together with the vitamin A, will prevent further infection and save the birds from certain death;
• In infected birds, with a camel's-hair brush, brush the pox blisters with 1% to 3% merbromin in 70% alcohol. (Use mercurochrome from Hynson, Westcott and Dunning, Inc., Baltimore, MD.);
• Take strict hygienic measures. A shallow trough containing sodium hydroxide should be placed outside the aviary entrance. Before entering, take off your shoes and put on rubber boots, and walk through the disinfectant. It is advisable to wear a lab coat and a hat or cap to cover your hair. These items of clothing should *stay in* the aviary afterwards; only your shoes stay outside;
• Aviary, utensils, etc. should be thoroughly cleaned and disinfected. Do not be frugal with the disinfectant (see page 65); use a new solution regularly, so that the disinfecting power is not reduced. After the disinfection of the aviary and its contents, everything should be rinsed well with clear water, then allowed to dry. Only then may healthy birds—after clearance by the veteranarian—be returned to the aviary.

Cere, Disorders of the: The cere is a fleshy and waxlike swelling at the base of the upper part of the beak in parrots, parakeets, and some birds of prey. In budgerigars, the cere is particularly prominent. Should the cere, which for example in a healthy green male budgie is blue, suddenly turn brown, there is a possibility that the bird is suffering from cancer of the reproductive organs—the testicles. If this is confirmed by an avian veterinary examination (this form of cancer can cause a greatly enlarged abdomen) then it is recommended that the bird be painlessly destroyed. To date there is no satisfactory cure for this affliction.

Sometimes the cere may color a dark or medium brown, following a loss of condition due to poor health or aging; this is known as brown hypertrophy or hyperplasia of the cere. The cere may grow additional layers of brown-colored skin and, if one does not take urgent action, there is a possibility that the nostrils will become blocked and a hornlike growth will develop.

Female budgies in particular, which by nature have a brown or pink cere, are susceptible to hypertrophy. The veterinarian should regularly remove the brownish buildup. It is important that you study the information on care and management; this can definitely lead to improvement.

The cere can also become infested with knemidokoptic mites (see Scaly Face and Scaly Legs, page 85), parasites which apparently develop entirely within the skin of their host, while feeding on keratin (the outer skin layer containing protein). It is also possible for tumors to develop in the cere area—in such cases, an avian veterinarian should also be consulted.

Coccidia: Coccidia are microscopic protozoan parasites which occur infrequently in budgerigars and lovebirds. They are spread in the droppings, consumed by the birds, and mature in the intestines. Ordinarily, they pose no danger to pet birds. They can be in the body for a long time before anyone notices. Consult your avian veterinarian if you notice a gradually decreased appetite, which is typically coupled with weight loss and loose droppings that may be somewhat bloody. These symptoms could signal a case of coccidiosis. If it is confirmed, sulfa drugs may be helpful. It is important to have recently imported birds checked for coccidiosis. Prevention depends on good hygiene and sanitation.

Cockatoo Syndrome: For some years we have known the devastating Psittacine Beak and Feather Symdrome (PBFS), sometimes named Cockatoo Syndrome. This disease manifests itself mainly among the so-called white cockatoos, and especially the molluccans. Recently it has also occurred among African gray parrots and various lovebirds, red rump parakeets, hooded parrots, Port Lincoln electus, rosellas, Bourke's mallee ringnecks, Princess of Wales, king parrots, malle-ringnecks, vasas, lorikeet species, cockatiels and budgerigars (parakeets).

It is probable that one or possibly two viruses are the causative pathogen of this disease. At the outset it is difficult to notice an infection, but a loss of feather powder, a dingy graying of the feathers in white cockatoos, retaining sheaths, and abnormal growth of the feathers are the first signs. The bird quickly gets the appearance of a feather-plucker. After these first symptoms, which gradually worsen, a loss of pigment in the beak and nails will follow, the growth rate of the beak will increase, and the upper mandible will grow over the lower. The sheaths are painfully curved. The whole condition of the bird worsens and it often becomes restless and moody. Pale spots appear in the plumage, and a gradual necrosis (death of living tissue) sets in on the inner edge of the beak. In the final stages, most of the feathers are diseased and various parts of the bird's body will be completely bald. The necrosis of the beak is so far advanced that pieces of the bill break off. If one touches the beak, the bird will feel pain. The bird acts neurotically, is usually very moody, and is extremely defensive.

It goes without saying that at the first suspicion of this disease an avian veterinarian should be consulted. Although the PBFS syndrome cannot be cured, secondary infections like lymphoma, bacterial infections, or tuberculosis (which often accompany PBFS syndrome) can be prevented with the appropriate medicines. Although no conclusive treatment has been discovered, various avian veterinarians are carrying out intensive research. In particular, Dr. Helga Gerlach of the University of

Diseases, Accidents, and Injuries

This cockatoo is seriously affected with PBFD, or Psittacine beak and feather disease.

Munich, West Germany, and Dr. Cathy A. Johnson, 1970 Sciber Lake Road 'L,' Lynnwood, WA, are researchers worthy of note. It is recommended that veterinarians who are insufficiently familiar with PBFS contact Dr. Johnson (telephone: (206) 775-0121). It is of utmost importance that the bird enthusiast be ever mindful of this disease; if PBFS is caught in its early stages, there is a good chance that something can be done for the patient.

Colds: Respiratory difficulties can come about from many causes, including drafts and low temperatures; exposure to various bacteria, fungi, and viruses; vitamin-A deficiency, and stress. You will notice that the patient has a rapid, audible respiration. The beak will be open, and the tail will bob. The bird may also sneeze and cough. It can have a nasal discharge, and will be off its feed. Often you will find the patient sitting quietly in a corner with ruffled feathers.

Place such a bird in a warm environment, and minimize stress. If there is a discharge from the nostrils, remove it carefully with a cotton ball. Use a vaporizer and spray a fine, warm mist of water into the cage to soothe and moisturize the inflamed lining of the respiratory tract. A standard vaporizer available at the drugstore is fine. Also, consult an avian veterinarian.

Conjunctivitis: This is an inflammation (most likely caused by bacteria, viruses, fungi, or physical irritants like dust, aerosol sprays, allergies) of the conjunctiva, the mucous membrane that lines the inner surface of the eyelid and the exposed surface of the eyeball. It occurs mainly in budgerigars, lovebirds, and other small parakeet species.

A similar complaint is *ophthalmitis*, which affects canaries and other small finches. Both diseases are closely related and infected birds rub their eyes constantly along the perch and blink profusely. Soon an ocular mucous discharge is apparent, which can be clear or pussy. If not treated in good time, ophthalmitis can lead to blindness. Conjunctivitis is somewhat easier and quicker to cure. Ophthalmic preparations, containing chlortetracycline (Aureomycin ophthalmic ointment, for example) can be used, usually with success. In general, these diseases are unpleasant and an avian veterinarian should be consulted.

Constipation: This is not a common complaint, but birds suffering from it will sit hunched up with spread feathers on the perch or on the floor and behave restlessly. Often the area around the vent is swollen. Birds can suffer this affliction after release into a cage or aviary when they may take too much gravel, too much egg food (which is usually too dry), or too much poppy seed. Also, bad or old seed can cause constipation, as can pressure on the rectum caused by hernia, tumor, or a retained egg. If bad food is the cause, it can happen that the vent is blocked by hard droppings. If the bird is dehydrated, it may not have enough fluid to produce liquid feces. Surprisingly, diarrhea can be a root cause of constipation, in that the droppings harden around the outside of the vent and the bird is then unable to defecate. By using a soft shaving brush, soft soap (baby soap, for example), and lukewarm water, the vent can be effectively cleaned. Do not use too much soap and water. This could spread over the rest of the plumage causing the bird to lose its insulation. However, a little can be safely applied around the vent.

Gastrointestinal upsets of one sort or another are commonly the reason for pet birds suddenly taking in excessive grit or other foreign objects and foods (compare this with dogs, which commonly eat grass when they have an upset stomach). Naturally, we should remove the grit and gravel in such cases and we can relieve the problem to some extent by giving extra green food, fruit, oil-soaked rape seed, or some orally administered mineral oil.

Antibiotics can be administered in the drinking water (ask the veterinarian for his advice). In serious or prolonged cases, an avian veterinarian should be consulted, especially as feces retained in the intestine for long periods will lose moisture and the bird will have great difficulty in passing them. By careful palpation of the abdomen, the veterinarian can give some relief to the patient. If a retained egg is the cause of constipation, then one should carry out the treatment described for egg binding (see page 75), but if one is not quickly successful, a veterinarian should always be consulted. Provided we feed and maintain our birds in the best possible way, constipation should seldom pose a problem.

Cysts: Canaries and budgerigars in particular are susceptible to feather cysts—especially in the wings, but also elsewhere. If found in their early stages, cysts can be surgically removed by the veterinarian. Benign cysts of the eyelid appear in pet birds from time to time and these can also be removed in a similar manner.

Dead-in-Shell: There are different and not always related reasons why an egg fails to hatch. In particular, a deficiency of the B vitamins and vitamin E before the breeding season begins can be a cause. A buildup of toxic substances in wild birds, for example DDT, is another cause (think of the many birds of prey!). Other causes can be such diverse things as too thick a shell; the bird sticking

to the inner membrane; incomplete incubation by the parents; sudden temperature variances and/or periods of drought, etc. A careful postmortem examination by a veterinarian can sometimes give an answer.

Diarrhea: Intestinal upsets in birds can be caused by a number of factors. One is poor food—poorly selected or in poor condition because of spoilage or contamination. Other possible causes are obesity, stress, respiratory or intestinal infection, excessive heat, or an excess of protein. Many bacterial and viral infections cause intestinal disturbances along with other symptoms.

Outward symptoms of impaired intestinal function are listlessness, hunched-up posture, and diarrhea. A case is serious when a bird will no longer rest on its perch and instead takes to the floor. It will sit in a corner with its head under its wing. The bird tends to drink quite a bit but will have little appetite, and its droppings are watery.

At this point it is best to call an avian veterinarian. Meanwhile, you can try home remedies. Personally, I have had good success with camomile tea. You may also give the patient boiled rice, oat flakes, and spray millet.

Intestinal disturbances can also occur if the weather turns quite warm and your aviary is poorly ventilated. Cold can be another cause. All extremes in temperature are a threat to the health of your birds!

Cold water is a special problem, particularly if the drinking dishes freeze in cold weather and your birds have to do without water for several hours. Lovebirds, unlike other parrots, drink a lot of water. So don't give parched birds water straight from the faucet, as they will drink too much cold water. Instead, provide it lukewarm. In general, lukewarm water should be the rule in winter.

Intestinal problems can be caused by poisoning from spoiled food or by contaminating substances. Be especially careful to avoid exposure to DDT and lindane in insecticides, as well as other chemical (aerosol) sprays!

Diseases, Accidents, and Injuries

If you suspect your pet birds have been poisoned, place them in a warm place and furnish fresh green feed and clean drinking water in which you have dissolved a little bicarbonate of soda. Another good purge is fresh milk or a few drops of Pepto-Bismol or Kaopectate. Never provide bicarbonate of soda for more than three days running, and always in low concentrations, such as 1 gram in 8½ ounces (.25 liter) of water.

A special type of poisoning occurs when birds get an excessive amount of protein, especially during the breeding season. Similarly, an excess of egg food and soft feed can bring on this problem. Often the breeder simply forgets that egg food should be provided in addition to, not instead of, the usual feed!

Affected birds suddenly show all the typical symptoms of poisoning. They seem dull and sleepy, they have trouble breathing, and they cease flying. Often they also develop severe diarrhea and can quickly die.

Be aware that diarrhea can be a symptom of a great number of avian diseases, but you don't have to suspect serious disease problems if you notice signs of diarrhea. If there are no other symptoms pointing to a specific illness, it can simply be a question of ordinary indigestion. For such cases, provide rice water instead of the usual drinking water, or use Norit. Dissolve a tablet of Norit in a tablespoon of water, and give the patient one or two drops in the beak, using a feeding syringe or a plastic medicine dropper.

A watery discharge isn't always diarrhea. Birds may react this way from fear, from being picked up by hand, or even from being observed too closely. Still, if you notice diarrhea, the safest response is to consult an avian veterinarian.

E. Coli Infections: Infections with *Escherichia coli* can pose serious problems for pet birds. *E. coli* principally infect humans, but birds are also quite susceptible.

Don't let anyone tell you that *E. coli* are normal residents of the bird's intestines. They can also easily spread to the lungs, liver, and heart, and can often lead to a speedy death.

The best preventive is good personal hygiene. Wash your hands before you move birds, prepare feed, inspect the nest, or carry out other activities with your birds. Prevent fecal contamination, and avoid spoiled food, dirty water, dirty perches, dirty nest boxes, dirty floors in cages and aviaries, and other sources of contamination.

Treatment consists of 3 to 4 drops of Kaopectate or Pepto-Bismol every 4 hours. Administer with a plastic medicine dropper. This will soothe and coat the inflamed digestive tract. Seek veterinary assistance if rapid improvement is not observed within 24 hours. There are a number of antibiotics that can provide relief, but they can be obtained only through a veterinarian.

Egg Binding: When birds are housed and fed properly, egg binding will be rare. Egg binding means that the bird cannot expel an egg that is ready to come out. The affected female looks sick, sits hunched up, moves little, and is easy to catch by hand in most cases. If you feel its abdomen, you quickly notice the trouble—the stuck egg. In the normal course of events, an egg spends no more than two hours in the cloaca and the wide section of the ovary leading to it. When it is ready, the muscles in the lowest part of the ovary move it into the cloaca, where it usually remains only a short time before it is pushed completely out of the body.

The muscles involved can fail to function properly as a result of infection or a vitamin deficiency. The bird will try valiantly to lay the egg, but in vain.

Another form of egg binding can result from shell-less or thin-shelled eggs (wind eggs). This condition can be caused by some malfunction in the deposit of calcium on the egg or by a calcium deficiency. The weak or absent shell tends to cause the egg to get stuck because the muscles in the ovary and cloaca can't get a good grip on the soft mass.

Normally egg binding can be avoided. Clearly, mineral and vitamin shortages must be prevented. Be sure that while the bird is breeding, it has an

Diseases, Accidents, and Injuries

ample supply of green feed and sprouted seed. To prevent wind eggs, be sure that your birds get enough calcium, particularly calcium phosphate. Commercial bird grit contains the key minerals, including calcium. Thus, you really don't have to do more than see to it that there is always plenty of calcium in the cage or aviary—grit, cuttlebone, mineral block.

Another way to avoid egg binding is not to start breeding too early in the season. Also, never breed females that are too young. Immature birds are extremely likely candidates for egg binding.

Egg binding is entirely curable, provided you act fast enough. First, use a plastic ear dropper to put a few drops of warm mineral oil in the vent (cloaca), so that the egg can be laid more easily. Second, transfer your patient to a hospital cage and raise the temperature to about 90°F (33°C) with an infrared lamp. Warmth and rest should help your bird to recover. I recommend, however, that you consult an avian veterinarian as soon as you notice any sign of egg binding.

Egg Pecking: Cage and aviary birds sometimes peck at eggs lying in the nest. Act immediately to remove the culprits from their living quarters. There is no known cause for egg pecking, but I am sure that the chance of its occurring is very small if you provide your birds with proper feeding, housing, and entertainment.

Enteritis: This is an inflammation of the small intestine. It is normally associated with diarrhea, and the greater part of the food (which cannot be digested properly) is passed in a watery state. It is not surprising that the feathers around the vent become greasy and dirty. The bird appears very sick, quickly loses weight, and—in the majority of cases—dies. The patient will drink abnormal amounts and has a great craving for grit. The bird should be immediately placed in a hospital cage at 90°F (32°C).

Enteritis is really a symptom of many diseases (salmonellosis, E. coli infection, coccidiosis, psittacosis, etc.), but it can be caused by other factors, such as unsatisfactory feeding, poison, tumors, various types of medications (!), even a change in the bird's environment or stress. Due to the seriousness of the symptoms, it goes without saying that an avian veterinarian should be consulted; he or she will attempt to diagnose the cause through laboratory tests. The patient is usually treated with a strong antibiotic. No grit should be given, but cooked oatmeal, boiled eggs (not too much), bread and peanut butter, and vegetable-type baby foods may be offered. To coat and soothe the inflamed digestive tract, Kaopectate or Pepto-Bismol can be administered. Be sure to follow the veterinarian's instructions carefully.

Eye Problems: Pet birds can be subject to several types of eye infections. In most cases, the problem results from complications from colds and other bacterial or viral infections. Other possible causes are a vitamin-A deficiency, the use of aerosol sprays, or dusty seeds that irritate the eyes.

A bird that has caught a cold in one or both eyes will close the affected organ. The eyes are teary and the edges inflamed. Bacterial infections often start from dirty perches, with the bird picking up the infection by wiping its beak along the perch. Another common cause is shipment of a large consignment in a small box, so look for trouble in recently imported birds. This type of infection causes the edges of the eye to be heavily inflamed—generally just one eye.

Place the patient in a warm environment, preferably in a hospital cage. Rinse the eye with 5% boric acid or apply an antibiotic ophthalmic ointment two or three times daily. (Neosporin or Neo-

Above left: The white java sparrow is a mutation.
Above right: The blue-gray colored java sparrow is the wild form. Java sparrows are sleek and hardy.
Below left: The red-headed finch or paradise sparrow is a fairly hardy species and often very prolific in captivity.
Below right: The hardy red-headed cardinal comes from Brazil, and is also called Pope and Dominican cardinal.

Diseases, Accidents, and Injuries

polycin are good commercial products.) A few days of treatment are usually sufficient to assure a speedy recovery. It is always wise to consult an avian veterinarian about the problem.

Knemidokoptes mites can also indirectly irritate eyelids and eyes when the typical scabs occur in this area. Treat the scabs with penicillin ointment and also treat the edges of the eye.

If there are wartlike little bumps on the lid, there may be a vitamin-A deficiency, which indicates the need to drastically alter the diet. At any rate, isolate a sick bird with these little bumps because they can also be a symptom of psittacine pox and this condition requires help from your veterinarian.

Serious causes of eye infection can lead to partial or complete blindness in one or both eyes. This is generally preceded by heavy tearing, after which the pupil turns milky white.

Birds that become partially or totally blind can be kept alive in a small cage. In the beginning, place food and water on the floor of the cage, preferably in a shallow earthenware dish. It takes a while for the blind bird to find its feed and water, although the learning process goes faster for a bird that has always been kept in a cage as compared to an aviary bird.

Feather Plucking: Some birds have the unfortunate habit of plucking their own feathers. This is especially common in large parrots such as macaws and African grays.

In the worst cases, a bird may pick itself completely bald, except for some sturdy wing and tail feathers and those on the top of its head that it can't

Above left: The Australian diamond dove will live peacefully with small finches in a garden aviary.
Above right: The hardy tambourene dove from Africa needs a secluded well-planted aviary.
Below: The Chinese quail is best housed in a garden aviary. There are various mutations, including silver, pied, and fawn.

An Elizabethan collar may be a last resort to control feather plucking.

reach with its beak. Lovebirds are often feather-pluckers; they may even pluck their young.

Many cases of feather plucking are difficult to explain. However, you can prevent most cases—and cure them as well—by giving birds something to do. To begin with, put a fresh willow branch complete with leaves into their cage every day. For finches and other small seed-eating birds, spray millet will do. Parrots and parakeets love to gnaw on willow branches. See to it that there is enough light in the cage, that it isn't too small or overstocked, that the temperature and humidity are right, and that each bird can take a bath every day. Birds should be able to bathe at any time of day, except in outside aviaries, where you should remove the bath water after 4 P.M. to permit the birds to go to sleep dry and not be exposed to chills.

Stress can be a major cause of feather-plucking. Another is insufficient rest. I have noticed that practically all cage birds require at least 12 hours of

Diseases, Accidents, and Injuries

sleep in a semidark cage or aviary. Birds that persist in their plucking can be provided with an "Elizabethan collar." They will get used to the device within a few days, although there are cases where birds don't want to have anything to do with it and keep trying hard to remove the collar. Such a collar cannot be used for small birds such as finches. Robert Altman, D.V.M., of New York, recommends unexposed X-ray film for the smaller bird: "A circle approximately 3 inches in diameter is cut out of the film; a slit is made from the edge of the circle to the center. A hole ½ inch in diameter is cut out of the center. This center opening should be slightly larger than the circumference of the bird's neck. The collar is placed around the bird's neck and the slit is closed with staples or tape. If tape is used, the strip of tape should be placed on the back of the collar so that the bird cannot chew and remove it."

Fractures: Fractures of the leg or wing can be avoided by handling birds gently and protecting them from barking dogs, prowling cats, and other animals. If accidents do happen, consult an avian veterinarian, especially if you are a beginning aviculturist.

If you treat a broken leg yourself, line up the severed sections and splint the fracture with a couple of thin sticks (for example, matches) on each side of the leg. Keep the splint in place by winding gauze around it and taping it with a piece of surgical tape. Wind the gauze tightly; you want to restrict the movement of the broken leg as much as possible. However, never wind the gauze too tightly. This can interfere with blood circulation, which can cause gangrene and even the loss of a limb.

Any bandage allows some movement. To avoid too much movement, I prefer an alternate method. I wrap the fractured leg with small strips of gauze that were previously treated with a thin preparation of plaster of Paris. First, wrap the leg twice, line up the leg properly, and wait until the plaster sets. Then wrap another couple of strips around the fracture.

It is harder to heal fractures that occur close to the body of the bird, and it may be especially useful

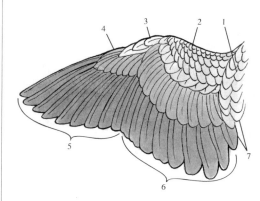

The wing:
1. Scapulars
2. Middle and lesser coverts
3. Spurious wing
4. Primary coverts
5. Primaries
6. Secondaries
7. Tertiaries

to use the gauze-plus-plaster method in these cases. In most cases, however, these tricky fractures require the skills of an avian veterinarian.

Some people talk of a broken leg when it really is a question of a torn muscle. This condition can occur when a bird makes desperate movements to free itself, for example, when caught in wire mesh, possibly because of overlong nails.

Torn muscles are difficult to heal. You can try to immobilize the injured leg with a bandage and keep it on while nature takes its course.

Birds with a leg injury should be kept in a hospital cage without perches until the healing process is complete. Cover the cage bottom with peat moss. Partially darken the cage and place it in a quiet location, so that the injured bird will move as little as possible. Be sure that its diet contains an adequate amount of vitamins (especially vitamin D) and minerals.

Broken, drooping wings can best be bandaged with gauze. Cut a slit in the gauze and put the folded wing through the slit. Then wrap the gauze around the body and secure it to a leg to keep it from sliding off. Make sure the bandage is tight without pinching the bird.

Wing fractures also call for placing the patient in a dark, quiet place for several weeks. Use a cage without perches that is low enough to assure that the bird won't attempt to fly.

Let me emphasize that setting a broken wing is a difficult task, and it's better to entrust it to a veterinarian. The treatment I suggested is likely to keep the wing in a proper position, but the bird may not be able to fly properly afterwards.

French Molt: Various young members of the psittacidae family, especially budgerigars and lovebirds, can be affected by French molt. Victims of this malady are commonly known as runners or creepers because their retarded growth and poor feathering prevent them from flying. The remaining primary flight and tail feathers are short and undeveloped, or are missing entirely, while the rest of the feathers, especially on the breast, are thin. There are no other obvious symptoms nor is there any loss in vitality. Creepers are active and alert and usually stay mobile by climbing around in their cages.

A microscopic examination of young feathers reveals that the follicle and quill have capillaries (small blood vessels) with extremely weak walls. The exact cause of the problem is unknown; a papovavirus is suspected but not definitely confirmed, despite considerable research.

At this time no good remedy has been found, even though scientists around the world are busy looking for one. Creepers should never be used for breeding. If you keep them around, feed them a varied diet high in protein at all times of the year.

Frozen Toes: Cold winter days pose the possibility of frozen toes. Lovebirds, various Australian parakeets and African finches, for example, can suffer from this problem by hanging onto the wire mesh too long, which they tend to do if they are suddenly disturbed. Similarly, if they sit on perches that are too thin they can run into problems because their toes are partially bare, not covered by feathers. Obviously, you need to replace the perches in such cases. If you use a sleeping cage, cover the bottom with a warm layer of peat moss.

If this problem occurs, there's not much you can do, much as I hate to say this. Often you do more harm than good. Consult an avian veterinarian, who could prescribe a salve.

The frozen part dries out and drops off without any apparent harm to the bird. Be sure that no infection occurs at that point. At the first sign of infection, treat the wound immediately with non-caustic iodine.

Goiter: Goiter, or enlargement of the thyroid gland, is particularly common among lovebirds, cockatiels, Australian grass parakeets (rosellas and Bourks, for example), and budgerigars.

Fortunately, this disorder no longer occurs often because commercial cage sand is often treated with iodine. The problem is still found, however, in areas where drinking water is deficient in iodine.

Usually goiter is not recognized by an external swelling. The growth, pressing against crop and windpipe, is internal. Clearly, any exertion such as flying or running will make the affected bird breathless very quickly. Breathing heavily, it will drop to the ground, often with widespread wings and pendulous crop and neck. It also might make a high-pitched squeak or wheezing sound with each breath.

In order to breathe more easily, the bird will often rest its beak against the bars of the cage or on a parallel perch or tree branch. If you fail to act immediately, the disease will worsen. Sudden death may follow due to suffocation, heart failure, or weakness due to insufficient intake of food.

In the case of a serious endocrinal disorder, give the bird iodine-glycerine. The proper mixture for budgerigars, lovebirds, and the like is 1 part iodine to 5 parts of glycerine; for larger parrotlike birds, 1 part iodine to 4 parts of glycerine. As an alternative, a mixture consisting of 9 parts paraffin oil to 1 part iodine-glycerine, administered with a plastic nasal dropper in a corner of the beak (for small, as well as for large parrots) intermittently over a period of three days, will work wonders.

Diseases, Accidents, and Injuries

Gout: This is a disturbance of the uric acid metabolism. There are two forms: visceral gout, in which the internal organs are affected and which is therefore difficult to diagnose; and articular gout, in which whitish, shiny, and hard swellings form around the joints of the legs, wings, and neck. In the latter form, the bird suffers acute pain and continually lifts its feet and spreads its wings. Although there is no direct treatment available, the condition can be improved by massaging and manipulating the affected parts under an anaesthetic—performed, naturally, by an avian veterinarian.

It will do no harm to increase the protein intake and to encourage the bird to take a multivitamin preparation. Drugs may be available which will alter the uric-acid levels. To prevent parrots in too-small cages from becoming afflicted with gout, perches of varying thicknesses should be provided. (Or better still, move the birds to larger quarters!) Naturally, you should see that food and water dishes are placed within the immediate reach of an infected bird. The chance of an infected bird becoming fully cured is rare, due to permanent kidney damage.

Heart Disease: It is obvious that the older the bird is, the more likely it is to have fainting fits, to collapse suddenly, and to finally die of heart disease. Fortunately it does not happen very often, but the veterinarian should be consulted the moment fainting fits occur. There are many different heart drugs available but diagnosis is difficult; the condition can, for example, be confused with liver and respiratory problems. Take care that the bird is never overweight and that it always receives a balanced diet.

Lice: Fortunately, cage and aviary birds are not often troubled with lice. Birds which are kept in garden aviaries, however, may occasionally be infested by wild birds. Infested birds have a "moth-eaten" appearance and frequently sit restlessly, continually pecking at their plumage and scratching their heads to relieve the skin irritation caused by these insects. If one examines the feathers of an infested bird with a magnifying glass, white oval specks may be observed. These are the clusters of eggs laid by the lice (lice spend their entire lives on the birds); the eggs are called "nits," and are normally laid in rows along the rachis (shaft). It is obvious that other birds in the same collection will soon catch the lice from an infested bird. An insecticide containing rotenone or pyrethrin (consult your veterinarian) can bring good results. In addition, cages, aviaries, nest boxes, and perches must be disinfested. The process should be repeated after 30 days.

Missing Feathers: Healthy feathers lie tightly against the bird's body. This is particularly noticeable in a bird that has just completed a molt and has

There are three types of feathers: Contour feathers (bottom), filoplume feathers (top) and down feathers (left). Contour feathers form the main plumage of the body, wing, and tail, giving the bird its shape and contour. Each contour feather consists of a long stem or rachis, which carries the vane with many barbs (see enlargement). Each barb has interlocking hooks and barbules.
Filoplumes are hairlike feathers with a thin rachis and a fluffy tuft at the tip.
Down feathers provide the insulation for temperature regulation, and have a short rachis and many noninterlocking barbs.

a whole new suit of feathers. Parrots, finches, and many other birds spend a lot of effort to maintain their appearance and groom their feathers with their beaks many times a day. It isn't hard, therefore, to notice if any feathers are missing. This can have a natural cause—as during the molt—or it can be a sign of trouble, indicating some type of illness.

Feather loss can be caused by improper feeding, a drafty environment, parasites, infections, metabolic and hereditary disorders, and other problems. If you notice any feather loss, investigate the cause first.

If your bird has any broken or split feathers, remove these or trim them back to keep the bird or its cagemates from picking at them. Such conditions often develop when birds are moved from one home to another, when they are caught, or as the result of scraps with other birds.

If feathers bleed, apply some hydrogen peroxide or styptic powder. Styptic powder burns the mouth, so be especially careful if you need to apply it near the beak. Bleeding in feathers that are still growing can be caused by fights, tight quarters, or excessive trimming.

Under no circumstances should you leave feathers lying on the bottom of the cage or the floor of the aviary. Loose feathers invite trouble because birds tend to pick at them (mainly out of boredom) and may develop an unhealthy interest in feathers.

Mites: See BALD SPOTS.

Molt: Many fanciers say that molt is a "healthy disease." This means, of course, that molt is not a disease at all, even if during molting birds show symptoms similar to a disease, such as a slight elevation in body temperature.

Molt is no mystery—it is the annual renewing of the bird's worn feathers. The old feathers fall out, and in a relatively short time new feathers grow in. These will have to last the bird until another year passes.

Be aware that the period of molt makes high demands on the bird's body. First of all, the bird loses heat when its feathers fall out. Secondly, there is a large amount of energy required to support a completely new growth of feathers in a relatively short time. In a sense, molting starts with nestlings, who replace their down with real feathers. These are their youth feathers, which remain for three or four months. Then the first real molt occurs, and the young bird gets its first adult feathers.

In adult birds, molt more or less signals the close of the breeding season. That season starts in the early spring with mating and brooding. A rest period follows, after which the bird gets ready for the next season. Molt is part of that preparation. It is initiated by the shorter day in fall, which triggers an increase in hormone activity. The feathers lose their elasticity and they drop out—fortunately, not all at once. Nature has arranged it so that a bird never loses so many flight feathers that it cannot fly (there are, however, some exceptions—for example, some ducks, geese, swans, etc.). First a few flight feathers drop; these are replaced by new ones before further flight feathers fall out, to be replaced in their turn. The loss of any type of feather is more or less balanced by the replacement of the same type of feather, so that a healthy bird is never bald during molt.

The period of molt requires extra care from you. First, take special precautions against having your birds catch cold. Second, make sure they have access to a protein-rich diet with plenty of vitamins (especially vitamins A and D) and minerals, and a rich assortment of green foods. Allow your birds as much rest as possible.

If you have indoor aviaries and cages, spray your birds with water at room temperature in the morning, or give them an opportunity to bathe. Bath water should also be furnished at room temperature.

With this type of care, the molt will proceed rapidly and smoothly, especially if you keep your birds in an outside aviary. The freedom of movement helps things along.

Abnormal molt can occur because of problems such as great changes in temperature, changes in light periods, and repeated stress or shock. Feather

Diseases, Accidents, and Injuries

regrowth is normally complete in six to eight weeks, depending on the bird species. If after that time the new feathers have not come in, there may be a problem with hormone imbalance. Be sure to consult an avian veterinarian. Then check the diet, housing, and hours of light provided; also watch for fights between birds. The veterinarian will check on whether the thyroid gland is functioning properly and whether a dietary supplement would help.

Nephritis: Nephritis or inflammation of the kidneys is unfortunately a frequently occurring disease of cage and aviary birds. The infected birds become lethargic and sit with ruffled feathers, often by the water dish, where they are likely to drink more than usual. As nephritis is often associated with other diseases, a consultation with the avian veterinarian is a necessity.

Newcastle Disease: This viral disease is highly contagious to poultry. It is possible, and has indeed several times happened, that an entire flock of birds has been destroyed in a few days. VVND (Velogenic Viscerotropic Newcastle Disease) can be encountered among all psittacine and passerine birds—although African parrotlike birds seem less likely to succumb to the disease. Mynah birds, canaries, weaver finches, and Java sparrows are, however, very susceptible, and of the named species, psittacines and mynahs are the most readily infected. Infected birds—which are usually, alas, unsavable—show paralysis of the legs; muscle-, eye-, and head-twisting; and often bloody diarrhea. To date, (as of 1989), there is no satisfactory treatment available. In any outbreak the government will become involved.

Should VVND be suspected, consult your avian veterinarian immediately. The strict quarantine laws pertaining to VVND (and psittacosis) should always be observed (see page 65).

Obesity: Birds that lack exercise because their cage is too small or because they haven't enough toys to keep them occupied may become fat. Birds that do not receive proper nutrition are also liable to fall victim to obesity.

Getting fat is, however, a very slow process. The owner must be alert and watch carefully for the first signs of obesity. When the bird can barely sit on its perch, things have already gone too far. The bird might sit on the bottom of its cage, lethargic and panting heavily. The contours of its body become blurred—heavy and cylindrical—and the skin appears yellowish when the feathers are blown apart. This is the fat shining through the skin, and the discoloration is apparent when you blow on the breast or abdominal feathers of such a bird.

Birds suffering from obesity live much shorter lives than those that have plenty of exercise and lively interests. The obese bird has difficulty molting and just sits, looking thoroughly bored.

The first thing is to give the birds plenty of exercise. Caged parrots and parakeets, for example, must be released daily in a secure area and allowed to fly freely for at least an hour. Birds receiving such daily exercise will never suffer from gout. Inside the cage or small aviary, birds must have even more exercise. Consider housing them in larger cages, or placing perches further apart. Hang some strong sisal ropes in the cages and a few bunches of spray millet or weed seeds. Many birds love to play with these seed sprays.

Next, improve the birds' nutrition and provide lots of well-washed greens and/or fruit. Avoid foods with high protein or fat content. Do not work on the assumption that "My bird is fat, so if I don't feed it for a few days it will be all right again." The bird must be fed, but with the right kind of food. It will perish, however fat it might be, if it receives no nourishment.

Pacheco's Parrot Disease: This viral disease is often encountered among psittacine birds in places where many are kept—quarantine stations, pet shops, etc.; in other words, where stress is a problem. The infected birds, which frequently have heavy diarrhea, die in a short time—from a few hours to a few days. The most likely cause of transmission of the disease is through food or water contaminated with the droppings of infected birds.

Diseases, Accidents, and Injuries

It is mainly Nanday and Patagonian conures that are suspected of being the primary carriers of this disease. To date, there is no satisfactory cure; even so, an outbreak should be immediately followed by a consultation with an avian veterinarian. There is one bright spot: The disease is not transmittable to man or poultry.

Poisoning: See DIARRHEA.

Psittacine Beak and Feather Syndrome: See COCKATOO SYNDROME.

Psittacosis: Psittacosis is the same illness in parrots and parakeets that is called ornithosis in other species of birds. It occurs only rarely in lovebirds.

This serious disease is caused by an obligate intercellular parasite, *Chlamydia psittaci*, which is distinguished from all other micro-organisms by a unique growth cycle. It occurs especially in dirty breeding operations and can be brought in by imported birds, especially smuggled ones. Be suspicious of dirty-looking birds. They may look utterly healthy, but a careful examination may reveal that they are infected.

Psittacosis can have a variety of symptoms and therefore is difficult to diagnose, especially in its early stages. Usually it starts with a heavy cold. Moisture drips from the nostrils, the bird gasps for air, and breathing is squeaky and hissing. It looks worn out and often has diarrhea. Before the disease turns fatal, there are often symptoms of cramps and lameness.

Psittacosis can occur in a mild form, which can often be completely cured. However, be aware that recovered birds can be infectious for both birds and man. Any case of the disease can pose a hazard, which is why you should report any suspicion of psittacosis to your veterinarian.

In humans, psittacosis starts with cold symptoms and can lead to a lung infection. In earlier times, the disease was dangerous. The advent of antibiotics has removed this danger, provided you get timely diagnosis and treatment. In the mid-1960s, many countries imposed strong restrictions on the importing of hookbills. Imported parrots have to be quarantined for 30 days on arrival, and are given a preventive treatment with chlortetracycline. Infected birds are treated for at least 45 days with this drug.

Runny Nose: If a bird should be continually snuffling and sneezing and is seen to have a runny nose (frequently the areas around the nostrils will be stained), it can be assumed that it is suffering from a respiratory infection. Shortly before such symptoms, it is possible that the voice will change (we humans get a sore throat or laryngitis) and from time to time a clicking noise will be heard as the bird breathes. Runny nose can be caused by an infection—fungal, bacterial, viral—but it can also happen that a bird sneezes due to a grain of sand or a seed stuck in the nostril. However, should a discharge be present, it is most likely that we are dealing with a respiratory problem. Aerosol sprays can also cause such problems. It should also be borne in mind that different kinds of nasal tumors can be a cause.

In all such cases it is advisable to consult an avian veterinarian. Should the trouble be caused by dirt, gravel, or seed, this can be carefully removed with the bristles of an old toothbrush. Aerosol sprays should be used with extreme care in the neighborhood of any bird accommodation.

In the event of respiratory disease, the veterinarian may administer antibiotics by mouth and/or by injection (tetracycline, chloramphenicol, tylocine, or gentocin). The patient should be moved to a quiet, warm place, especially out of drafts! One should ensure that the bird eats and drinks well and receives extra tidbits to encourage a quick recovery.

Scaly Face: Scaly face is caused by mites (*Knemidokoptes pilae*). These attack the area around the eyes and beak, and in serious cases, the legs and toes. These insectlike parasites burrow passages in the top layers of the skin, where they lay their eggs. If left untreated, the rough scales that result grow steadily worse and serious deformities of the beak can occur. The condition spreads from

Diseases, Accidents, and Injuries

one inhabitant of the aviary to another if action is not taken.

The crusty scales can be treated with vaseline or glycerine. You can also use mineral oil, but be careful to daub it on the infected area only and don't drip oil on the feathers. In difficult cases, consult your avian veterinarian. He or she may treat the affected areas with Eurax Cream or, in serious cases, with Ivermectic (Equalan), an injectable medication.

Remove any scabs that fall off as quickly as possible and burn them if you can. Then avoid further infestation by cleaning the cage, perches, sleeping cages, and nest boxes. Scaly face is not a dangerous infection, but it is a pesky one that merits great care to be sure it is completely eradicated.

Sore feet: Sore feet may be caused by a torn nail, fractures, various infections, toe dislocation, gout, burns, or lack of proper exercise. Ensure that the nails never grow too long. By using perches of various thicknesses, many problems will be averted. Broken or overgrown nails must be clipped (see page 41). Naturally, all birds must have the daily opportunity to exercise properly, perhaps freely in the room (for precautions, see page 37) or in roomy cages or aviaries. In addition, ensure that perches are not too rough and are not covered with droppings or other mess. Wet perches also create problems, such as rheumatism. If the bird's feet and legs appear red and swollen, bathe them in warm water for about 5 minutes, dry them with a soft cloth, and apply a very thin layer of skin ointment. Ensure also that the bird is not suffering from a deficiency of calcium, phosphorus, vitamins (especially D_3), or protein; these nutrients are especially important during the breeding season.

Stress: Stress is a condition that brings the bird's defense mechanism to a state of high readiness. In order to counter stress the bird must use its bodily reserves. But when its reserves are depleted, the bird weakens; resistance becomes low, and the bird is likely to become ill. The main causes of stress in pet birds include:

Feet and claws are very important. Legs and toes are covered with a protective layer of scales. The claws are thin in finches, thick in parrots, but always sharp and curved for climbing, perching, and walking. From top left, clockwise: Java sparrow, dove, Amazoparrot, and cockatoo.

- Transport
- New home/New owner
- New family member or visitor
- Bird shows
- Excessive noise—television, vacuum cleaners, mixers, etc.
- New noises
- Long training sessions
- Sexual frustration
- Overcrowding
- Caging and handling by untrained people
- New cage location
- Any environmental changes, including: Temperatures less than 60°F (15°C) or greater than 90°F (32°C); Too much darkness—greater than 15 hours a day; Too much daylight—greater than 15 hours a day.
- New food or change of feed cup position
- Boredom
- Other pets staring into the cage or harassment from other birds and pets, as well as from humans.

Diseases, Accidents, and Injuries

- Diseases
- Poor nutrition

Ticks: See BALD SPOTS.

Worm Infestations: Parakeets, gallinaceous birds, and waterfowl in particular can have worm problems which, unless treated urgently, can be fatal. There are two groups of parasitic worms that concern us and these include those that feed on the contents of the gut and others that are found in the respiratory tract. We can divide worm infestations into the following types:

- Roundworm or *Ascaridia* infestation
- Threadworm or *Capillaria* infestation
- Tapeworm or *Taenia* infestation
- Gapeworm or *Syngamus* infestation

Roundworm (*Ascaridia hermafrodita*) is largely a parasite of parakeets and different kinds may be found in Australian and South American parakeets. In pigeons and doves, the species *Ascaridia columbae* may be found. The damage caused by roundworms can sometimes be considerable. When fully grown, the parasites can measure 1½ inches (4 cm) long and 1 mm thick. Not only do they damage the lining of the gut—mainly while they are still in the larval stage—as they collectively attack the glands that produce the intestinal juices, they also consume the nutrients from the food that the bird has eaten.

They multiply very quickly, so that stoppage in the gut is very likely and there is a possibility that they will encroach in the gall duct, thus causing damage to the liver. Adult worms periodically lay eggs which are passed out in the birds' droppings. Once in the open, these eggs can withstand wide ranges of conditions, including cold and dryness, but in a prolonged drought or in constant, direct sunlight, they will be destroyed. At moderate temperatures and humidity levels, the embryos develop and the eggs become infestatious. Should a bird accidentally ingest such an egg, a larval worm will

hatch and feed upon the contents of the bird's gut. The period from larva to adult worm is about 25 days, sometimes a few days more or less.

In minor cases of infestation, it is not possible to see any change in the health of the bird, but a regular microscopic examination of the bird's droppings will indicate whether a roundworm infestation is present in the aviary. In more serious cases, in the early stages the bird will gradually begin to lose weight and condition.

As the infestation worsens, not only will the bird lose more weight, frequently a paralysis of the feet will develop; sudden death is not unlikely, caused by a total compaction of the bowel due to the worms, in either adult or larval form. It is possible that a stoppage can be caused by worm larvae alone; an infestation may arise from eggs picked up while feeding. Unfortunately, there is no way of diagnosing a roundworm in the bird or in its droppings until 20 to 22 days after the first infestation.

A good vermicide will bring relief; for example the veterinarian may recommend Piperazine or Ripercol-L (the latter is injectable levamisole). The European Fenbendazol can be administered in drops to the beak, or added to fruit or egg food. These vermicides are effective against both round- and threadworms. An excellent treatment against tapeworm is Yomesan. All are supposedly safe medicines even when slight overdoses are administered. (But don't think that if a little is good, a lot is better. Deliberate overdosing can be harmful.)

In cases where the infestation is in more advanced stages, it is advisable to worm the whole stock of birds as soon as possible. The birds' accommodation should be disinfected; in the outside aviary, the earth should be turned over to a depth of 20 inches (50 cm) and covered with a layer of new sand. It is very important to keep the floor dry, to prevent the further development of any eggs. The earth can also be treated with a solution of Natron or soda-lye disinfectant—consult your veterinarian. Parakeet fanciers frequently encounter worm problems, and it is recommended that they regularly send feces samples of their birds for microscopic examination.

Threadworms (*Capillaria*) may be encountered in most bird species. They are round, threadlike parasites that live in the ground as larvae and from there are ingested by the birds. The parasites grow to maturity in the crop or in the small intestine. The adults lay eggs, which are passed out in the droppings. Infested birds lose weight and develop diarrhea. Frequently the infested bird may have difficulty in swallowing. Piperazine or Levamisole (as prescribed by your avian veterinarian) may also be used here. If an infestation is suspected, an immediate fecal examination is necessary. The aviary should be disinfected in the manner described for roundworms.

Tapeworm (*Taenia syngamus* or *T. cestodes*) is seen most often in the African Gray Parrot. There are tapeworms which can be transmitted by a vector—such as flies, molluscs, beetles—and infect the birds. The worms are parasites of the small intestine where they attach themselves to the gut wall, so that they are not moved by peristaltic action. In the intestine, the worms develop to adulthood by the continual production of segments (*proglottids*). The segments become full of eggs and, as soon as they are ripe, they break free and are passed out with the bird's droppings. One of the above-mentioned transport hosts takes up the eggs and the process starts again from the beginning.

Infested birds quickly weaken and develop diarrhea, but there are also birds that show no obvious symptoms. In addition to keeping out the vector species, treatment from the veterinarian is recommended; an excellent remedy is Yomesan. Cages and aviaries should be kept clean and regular fecal examinations should be carried out.

Gapeworms (*Syngamus*) can infest any bird but are fortunately rare. The worms are red, Y-shaped and infest the respiratory tract. The larvae are often picked up directly by the birds or via a transport host, such as earthworm or snail. The worm lays its eggs in the trachea and in time, these are coughed up

and can be picked up by another bird. The worms migrate to the respiratory tract from the intestines. An infested bird evinces labored breathing, with coughing and gaping, and the neck is frequently stretched out to make breathing easier. An avian veterinarian will prescribe something like thiabendazole. Excellent hygiene in the bird's accommodation will limit the chance of infestation, but if you suspect a case, the droppings should be examined for eggs. With large birds, like African grays, it is possible to swab the trachea to make a positive diagnosis.

Wounds: Wounds can be caused by fighting or by aggressive colleagues in the aviary, and of course through other accidents. When a bird is bleeding, it should be caught immediately and placed in a quiet spot for treatment. In addition to its normal menu, supply extra treats and a few drops of a good vitamin/mineral preparation in the drinking water. The three most common kinds of bleeding arise from:

• Skin wounds. Take a sterile gauze and apply firm, steady pressure. When the wound stops bleeding it should be cleaned. Use a good pair of forceps to remove debris, such as feathers or dirt. The wound is best dabbed with a solution of hydrogen peroxide; endeavor to avoid scrubbing and probing as this will only start bleeding afresh.
• Bleeding nails and/or beaks. See page 41.
• Bleeding feathers. Many birds, especially parrots and parakeets, peck at their feathers during the molt. Growing quills are filled with blood and, should these be damaged, profuse bleeding can result. The blood in quills does not clot readily, so action should be taken immediately. Pull out the feather shaft completely—use forceps. Should the follicle continue to bleed, apply pressure to the outside of it for 2 minutes. It is often necessary to clean away the blood first with a sterile pad, in order to see where the wound is situated. Work as quickly as possible, as many birds cannot suffer loss of blood without suffering from shock. It is best to perform this little

Diseases, Accidents, and Injuries

operation yourself, rather than consult a veterinarian—the time lost may be fatal to the patient. Such a case must be treated quickly (see coagulant products, page 83). As soon as the bleeding has stopped, the patient should be placed in a large cage, in a quiet, shady spot. Keep at a temperature of 80° to 85°F (26°–29°C). Should the patient become weak or paralyzed, or have difficulty breathing, the veterinarian can then be called immediately.

Equipment and Supplies

Although serious illness or accidents almost always require the advice and care of an avian veterinarian, you will be better equipped to cope with emergencies if the following items are available:

• Heat source. Infrared lamp (60-to 100-watt bulb); heating pad.
• Hospital cage. Several commercial models are available. Ask your veterinarian or pet-store manager for advice.
• Environmental thermometer. Buy one that's easy to read, so that you can accurately monitor the temperature in the hospital cage.
• Adhesive or masking tape. Use ½-inch width.
• Gauze bandage. Use ½-inch roll.
• Sterile gauze pads, cotton-tipped swabs (Q-tips), rubbing alcohol, needle-nosed pliers or tweezers, sharp scissors with rounded ends.
• Feeding tubes. Use 8F or 10F tubes, which many avian veterinarians carry. Ask him or her to demonstrate the technique of tube feeding. Syringes or plastic medicine dropper for oral administering medication.
• Clorox. In a dilution of 6 ounces (177 ml) per gallon (3.8 L) of water, excellent for cleaning concrete floors, but may be corrosive to bare metal.
• Gevral Protein. For appetite loss. Always mix with Mull Soy, which is also a good source of essential vitamins and minerals. Use 1 part Gevral Protein to 3 parts Mull Soy; tube feed 2 to 3 ml 2 to 3 times daily. Ask your avian veterinarian for more details.
• Kaopectate or Pepto-Bismol. For loose droppings and regurgitation. Soothes and coats the digestive tract. Helps to form a solid stool. Dosage: 2 to 3 drops every 4 hours, administered with a plastic medicine dropper.
• Karo Syrup. For dehydration and as a provider of quick energy. Add 4 drops to 1 quart (1 L) of water. Administer 8 to 10 drops slowly in the mouth every 20 to 30 minutes with a plastic dropper.
• Maalox or Digel. For crop disorders. Soothes the inflammation and eliminates gas. Dosage: 2 to 3 drops every 4 hours.
• Monsel Solution. For bleeding. Don't use styptic powder for areas near the beak.
• Milk of magnesia. For constipation. Dosage: 3 to 5 drops in the mouth with a plastic dropper, twice daily for two days. Don't use milk of magnesia if your bird has kidney problems or heart disease. Consult your avian veterinarian.
• Mineral oil. Constipation, crop impaction, egg binding. Dosage: 2 drops in the mouth for two days with plastic dropper. Be very careful when administering the oil as it can cause pneumonia if it enters the breathing tubes and lungs.
• Goodwinol, mineral oil, Scalex, Eurax, Vaseline. Scaly face and/or scaly legs and feet.
• Betadine, Domeboro Solution, A & D Ointment, Neosporin, Neopolycin, Mycitracin, Aquasol A. For skin irritations. Domeboro is used on wet dressing: Dissolve 1 teaspoon or 1 tablet in a pint of water. A & D is excellent remedy for small areas. Neosporin, Neopolycin, and Mycitracin contain antibiotics. Aquasol A is a cream and contains vitamin A. All these ointments and creams can be applied to the affected skin twice daily.
• Lugol's Iodine Solution. For thyroid enlargement. Dosage: ½ teaspoon of Lugol with 1 ounce of water. Place 1 drop of this mixture in 1 ounce of drinking water for 2½ weeks.

Selected Popular Pet Birds

The emphasis in this gallery of cage and aviary birds is on breeding, although detailed information regarding care and management is, if applicable, also provided. The following groups of birds are considered.

Canaries: This section deals (in layman's terms) with canaries in general—including song and color varieties. Under the influence of feeding, housing, and cross-selective breeding, the wild canary (*Serinus canaria*), originally from the Canary Islands, went through various mutations. Some of these varieties, like the roller, gloster, border and red-factor canary, are excellent birds for the beginner. All require essentially the same care and management, as indicated in the introduction to this entry. Larger breeds, however, such as Yorkshire and Norwich, are best left until you have gained some experience. Nevertheless, detailed information on the different varieties of type canaries is provided to assist you in identifying the various breeds and making an intelligent choice.

Budgerigars or Parakeets: This section provides straightforward advice on how to keep and breed these birds, which, because of their enormous popularity, are introduced separately in spite of the fact that they are actually a small species of parrot (see below). Whether you want one of the more common color varieties in your house or a more unusual breed for your garden aviary, you will find this information helpful. There is, by the way, no truth in the story that some color varieties are easier to teach or to breed than others. Thus, your decision is simply a matter of which color and markings you like best.

Parrots and Parrotlike Birds: Various species are available at most times of the year, but supplies tend to be more plentiful during midsummer and after the breeding season. After a general introduction, popular species are presented with emphasis on breeding data that differs from that given in the introduction to this entry.

There is often confusion regarding the names *parakeet* (sometimes spelled *parrakeet*), *parrot*,

Various nest boxes. Top left clockwise: closed nest box for lovebirds and parakeets (budgerigars); closed nest box for parakeets; half–open nest box for finches; log nest for parrots and large parakeets; grandfather clock nest box for large parrots and parakeets; and closed nest box with a removable concave bottom.

parrotlike birds, psittacines, etc. All hookbills of the family *Psittacidae*, regardless of size, color, or place of origin, are *parrots*; hence lovebirds, cockatiels, conures, macaws, and parakeets are all *parrots*. The name parakeet was given by aviculturists to the smaller species of parrots. All in all, parrots are a very homogeneous group, so a general introduction is appropriate.

Finches and Related Seed-eating Birds: This is a relatively homogeneous bird group which, in general, requires the same care and management as parrots. Therefore the entry starts with a general introduction, followed by a description of many colorful representatives of this interesting family.

Quail and Doves: These two entries deal with the most important and familiar species, which are treated in the introduction itself.

Soft-billed Birds: This section presents some difficulties. Soft-billed birds—a far from homogeneous group—can be loosely defined as non-seed eating birds. They include omnivores such as mynahs and toucans, frugivores such as touracos, nectivores such as sunbirds and hummingbirds, insectivores such as woodpeckers and flycatchers, and carnivores such as hornbills and the majority of shrikes. Never think that the beak of a so-called soft-bill is physically softer than those of its seed-eating hard-billed relatives. It is easy to understand that the fragile-beaked hummingbird is regarded as being a soft-bill. But what about a woodpecker with a bill hard enough to hammer through a tree? Obviously, therefore, the introduction to this section deals only with general information, followed by rather detailed descriptions of the various bird species.

Canaries

The breeding of canaries poses few problems, providing we create the correct conditions. The best time to begin breeding is roughly the middle of April. The young will then hatch at the beginning of May, when the temperature is usually high enough to prevent the hatchlings from chilling, should the hen no longer brood them at night. Remember that the young from the first brood of the season are usually the best and if you start breeding too early, there is a danger of losing them due to low temperatures.

If you allow the birds to breed in a room aviary, it is advisable to provide the same number of nest pans as there are hens. It is even better to provide a couple of extra ones to allow them a choice. Canary hens are like other female birds—they find it difficult to choose. The number of birds will naturally depend on the size of the garden or room aviary. In a medium-sized cage, you can keep one cock with two or three hens, but a room aviary is usually large enough to hold three or four cocks and up to twelve hens. Without a few small squabbles and bickering, a good social atmosphere will never prevail; nor is

it possible to tell which cock has mated with which hen. If you want to breed your birds systematically, you are advised to use breeding cages. Breeding cages in various forms and makes are available from pet stores, but with a little skill, the home handyman can easily make his own more economically from thin plywood. The wire fronts, with which the do-it-yourselfer would have the most difficulty, can be purchased from avicultural suppliers. These cage fronts are complete with doors and brackets for food and drink containers.

Ideally, the cage should be built of ample size, to allow it to be divided in half with a central sliding panel. A small hole is left in the panel, small enough to prevent a bird from getting through. The young from the first brood which are still dependent can then be kept in one half of the cage when the hen starts on her second clutch, but she can still feed them through the hole in the panel.

Should the birds not be in breeding condition, the divided cage can still be useful. The female is placed in one side of the breeding cage and the cock in the other. After a couple of days, the hen is provided with her nest pan and nesting material, consisting of fine hay and grass about 2 inches (5 cm) long, and wool, raffia, and pieces of soft, unraveled string of similar length. As soon as the nest is ready, the cock is let in with the hen and pairing should soon take place. Squabbles between the cock and the hen may occur with this method. Should you wish to take advantage of the fact that the cock is capable of fertilizing four hens, then make a cage with three compartments, the one in the center being smaller than the others. Put the cock in the middle compartment and two hens in each of the outer compartments. As soon as the hens have their nests ready, the cock is introduced first to one pair of hens, then to the other so that they may all be fertilized. If this is successful and all hens start brooding, you can allow the cock to stay with two of the hens, where he will soon be busy feeding his two wives, and later on helping with the foraging of the youngsters. The other two hens must look after themselves and their young with no extra help, which will mean that broods of the latter will not develop as quickly as those reared with the assistance of the father.

In order to gain extra space it is best not to place nesting baskets inside the cage but to use the so-called Harzer nest boxes which are hung outside the cage. A hemp or string nest, which can be obtained from your local pet store, is placed inside the box along with a suitable quantity of other nesting material as described above. The floor of the breeding cage, just like that of every other cage, should have a sliding tray with a layer of sand on it. Before nesting begins, the nest box and the nest should be sprayed with a safe insecticide to kill lice.

During the breeding season canaries must be able to bathe. The water should be at room temperature and therefore must not be given straight from the tap. The incubation period of canary eggs is about 13 days and the average clutch contains 5 eggs, laid at intervals of 24 hours. It is best to remove each egg as soon as it is laid and to replace it with a dummy egg, available at your pet shop. After the last egg is removed, the dummy eggs are replaced with the real eggs, which have been stored in a can on cotton wool placed over dry sand, preferably with the pointed end down; *gently turn the eggs over daily.* The advantage of this method is that all eggs will hatch at approximately the same time.

The main food for canaries consists of rape seed, together with canary-grass seed, millet, broken oats, niger seed, linseed (flax), lettuce seed, and hemp (if available) or teazle (see page 43), as well as the all-important green food. At the beginning of the breeding season, start to give egg food in small quantities, so that the birds grow accustomed to it. If you do not do this, there is a chance that this essential supplement will be withheld from the young. Egg foods are available from pet stores in various brands. Always choose the best, even if it is a little more expensive. Or you can prepare your own, so that you know precisely what your birds are

A canary requires a shallow bowl and fine grass as nesting material.

getting. A suitable food can be prepared with a hard-boiled egg, mixed together with two rusks, a teaspoon of honey, a pinch of dicalcium phosphate, and a little poppy seed. The eggs and rusks are mashed as fine as possible, so that the ingredients can be thoroughly mixed. This rearing food must be prepared fresh each day and given to the birds at least twice a day. You can also add a little finely grated carrot or chopped spinach to the mixture, taking care that neither has been treated with herbicide or insecticide. Ensure that the birds have a permanent supply of cuttlefish bone. Unless the youngsters are sick, or the rearing food is wrongly put together, the hen will rarely neglect her young. If this should happen, it can also be caused by the temperature in the breeding room, which should be approximately 65°F (18°C). As you are probably aware, young canaries come into the world almost naked and are at first brooded by the hen for most of the day. She leaves the nest only to relieve herself, to eat, or to collect food for the chicks. If the chicks are too chilled when she returns, they will be too weak to open their beaks—and it is this action which stimulates the feeding response in the hen. If the beaks remain shut, the hen will make no attempt to feed the chicks and, in a short time, will leave the nest completely. It is possible to hand-rear a nest of chicks that have been abandoned, but this is difficult and time consuming. If you have other nests of chicks at the same time, the young may be distributed among these for fostering. This is one of the reasons for not starting the breeding until at least the middle of April.

Within 14 days, the chicks will have developed most of their plumage, will resemble their parents, and will be recognizable as canaries. They can have leg bands (2.9 mm) fitted after the sixth day. Banding should not be delayed too long, for it will then become impossible. If there are difficulties, smear a little petroleum jelly on toes and foot (see illustration, page 122). It is advisable to do the banding just before the birds retire for the night. You will then avoid the slight chance that the hen will attempt to remove the rings from the nest and, in so doing, throw out one or more chicks. At dawn the following day, the hen will be more occupied and is less likely to be worried by the rings. A preventive measure to take is to blacken the bands with a felt-tip pen, so that they're less shiny. Also, rub some droppings on them, to give them a familiar scent. Ordinarily, this will make the rings less objectionable and the canary hen may leave them alone.

At three weeks, the young will leave the nest and begin to peck at the rearing food themselves, though their beaks are still likely to be too weak to crack the husks of hard seeds. Therefore, they should be given 2 daily supply of softened rape seed. This can be done by pouring hot water over the seed, allowing it to soak for a while, then draining and drying it with a cloth. If you do not take this precautionary measure there is a possibility that a chick will sit all day long with a seed in its beak without actually eating it—this will, of course, retard its development.

As soon as the young are independent—usually by the thirtieth day—new nest material should be provided, otherwise there is the chance that the hen will pluck feathers from the chicks. As soon as she starts on a new clutch, the first chicks should be separated into another compartment, but one where the cock can still feed them through the partition.

Unlike parakeets (budgerigars), zebra finches and society finches, domestic canaries retain their natural cycles and do not breed throughout the year. From July to February, during which time the molt also occurs, the cock and the hen show little interest in each other and can be safely left together. The young birds usually begin to molt in August and renew all their feathers with the exception of the tail and flight feathers. These are changed along with all the other feathers at the second molt, which occurs about one year later. It is important to remember that the molt is a difficult time for birds and is an exhausting process for their bodies (see page 83). Additional care is therefore essential at this time. Normally, the molt takes three to four weeks to complete and should go so smoothly that the only sign is the feathers at the bottom of the cage. The molt begins with the tail and flight feathers, but nature sees to it—at any rate with the canary—that not all flight feathers are lost at the same time so that the bird can fly. The molt usually begins with the outer flight feathers. The last feathers to molt are those of the head. During the molt you must ensure that the birds are not exposed to drafts, nor should there be sudden changes in temperature. They should also have the possibility of taking a daily bath. The need for calcium and various vitamins during the molt is the same as the requirements during the breeding season.

Form and Posture Canaries

The Belgian Bult Canary: This is one of the oldest varieties of canary in the world. Its origin is not entirely clear, but it is presumed that it evolved from the Mechelse waterslager. The arched back can still be found in this song canary. Through mutation, selection, and adjustment, the water-slager eventually evolved into the Belgian bult.

The "place of birth" of this bird was most likely Ghent and surrounding areas. The breed is sup-

Canary silhouettes, idealized. Left to right: Lancashire coppy, Belgian bult (in "work" position), and Scotch fancy.

posed to have been perfected during the sixteenth century.

Belgian bults were used extensively in the creation of many other canary breeds, including the frills, the Yorkshire, the Lancashire, and the Scotch fancy. It is obvious that the posture of this bird is quite ordinary. Only through intensive training will it adopt the show position with its neck fully extended and its body erect.

Characteristics:

• *Head:* small, sleek in shape, giving a "snaky" appearance.

• *Neck:* long, thin, and elongated.

• *Shoulders:* high, but not giving a bony appearance; in other words, well filled.

• *Back:* long, broad, and vertical.

• *Body:* long, narrow, with high shoulders.

• *Breast:* well filled and thrust forward.

• *Wings:* long and closed; the wings should touch each other without crossing over.

• *Tail:* straight down, long, and closed.

• *Legs:* long, stretched out, and with well-feathered thighs.

• *Plumage:* smooth and without frills; closed; the breast feathers may stick out just a little due to the build of the bird, and this cannot be avoided.

• *Length:* 6½ to 7 inches (17–18 cm) from the tip of the tail to the tip of the beak.

• *Position:* the best bird is the one that looks like a figure 7 when it is placed in the training cage. It should stand high on its legs, with the neck slightly lowered. The tail should barely touch the perch. *

The Bernese Canary: This posture canary is the Swiss national canary. Although carrying the name of Switzerland's capital, it was not necessarily developed there, as a canary often inherits the name of an area or town, such as the Norwich and Yorkshire canaries. The Swiss wanted a race that would stand out for its proud posture and slender form, and it was to be as pure as the Swiss Alps themselves. After years of hard work, Switzerland had its own canary breed, a bird that stands very tall and erect, is still somewhat stocky, but nevertheless makes an attractive impression.

Characteristics:

• *Position:* well proportioned, elegant, and reasonably corpulent. The posture should be very erect and proud.

• *Length:* 6¼ to 6¾ inches (16–17 cm).

• *Head:* short and broad with a short, flattened skull.

• *Neck:* quite long and thick.

• *Breast:* well developed and massive.

• *Wings:* long and closed; tips should not overlap.

• *Shoulders:* sturdy and well marked.

• *Tail:* long, narrow, and forming one line with the back.

• *Legs:* long, with a slight bend at the heels.

---

* The characteristics of each variety and the order in which they are listed are determined by officials of the respective breed society.

Selected Popular Pet Birds

Canary silhouettes, idealized. Top: Gloucester corona (left) and Norwich (right); bottom: border (left) and Parisian frill (right).

• *Plumage:* full, smooth, and fine.
• *Color:* one color or variegated; must be quite shiny.

The Border Canary: This breed originated in or around 1891 along the border of England and Scotland, hence the name. Because of its length, only 5 inches (13 cm), it was called the "wee gem." Through the years the size of the border canary has increased to 6 inches (15 cm).

Characteristics:
• *Position:* erect, relaxed, with wings laying flat and closed.
• *Length:* 5½ to 6 inches (14–15 cm).
• *Plumage:* close, silky, and smooth.
• *Form:* nicely rounded head, straight line from back to tail; somewhat rounded throat; flowing roundness from breast to stomach.
• *Wings:* well closed.
• *Legs and feet:* medium length; only a small part of the thighs should be visible.

• *Tail:* tail feathers should be fairly close together; tail should be slender.
• *Color:* soft but varied.
• *Condition:* healthy and lively, without faults.

The Crested Canary: The origin of this breed is somewhat mysterious. By using the Mechelse waterslager, Mr. F. W. Barnett, from Falkenham, Norfolk, England, developed a crested canary which became known as the "King of the Fancy" toward the end of the last century.

There are two types of crested canaries: crest and crest-bred, which carries the plain head. In order to breed proper offspring, it is essential to pair crest to plainhead—as should be done with all crested canary varieties. (If two crested canaries are mated, they produce, genetically, three types of chicks: crest-bred, single-factor crest, and double-factor crest. The latter is not viable.)

Characteristics:
• *Crest:* as large as possible, consisting of broad feathers that form a well-radiating circular crest, the center of which is preferably in the center of the head. The crest should be as flat as possible, but without interruption, even on the neck. Dark crests are preferred.
• *Beak:* fine and narrow.
• *Neck:* well filled.
• *Body:* looks like that of a goldfinch, with full breast and broad back. Soft, thick, and broad feathering; flank feathers of the crested canary can measure up to 2¼ inches (6 cm).
• *Legs:* short and smooth.
• *Tail:* short and slender..
• *Wings:* the tips may not fall over the rump; they should be touching but not overlapping.
• *Position:* the imaginary line the bird should parallel would be a 45° angle.
• *Color:* one color, preferably with melanin-colored crest.
• *Condition:* healthy and lively.

We would like to emphasize here again that crest × crest will produce a lethal factor of 25%. We therefore recommend crest × crest-bred.

Selected Popular Pet Birds

The Gibber Canary: The Italian humpback frill, or gibber italicus as it is known on the Continent, is identical in shape to the southern Dutch frill (see page 99) and belongs to the frilled posture canary group. The southern Dutch frill has no doubt played a role in the development of the form of the Gibber canary, which is, however, a smaller bird. It has maintained the nervous nature of the southern Dutch frill.

The gibber is really the end result of erroneous breeding! Continuous breeding of intensive or non-frosted birds caused the feathers to become more and more sparse, to the point where the breast and thighs ended up bald. (Intensive red, intensive gold, etc. applies to birds with this type of feather, regardless of the color series to which the breed belongs.) The small size can also be blamed on the intensive factor. But it is just this nakedness of the thighs and breast that makes a good Gibber! It stands to reason that only experienced breeders have success in breeding this somewhat strange-looking canary, because a certain insight and intuition is required to enable a breeder to know just how far the intensive factor can be bred. Many chicks die before or just after coming out of the egg or when they are still very young.

Characteristics:
• *Head and neck:* "snaky," small head and beak. The neck carried in a horizontal position. Both head and neck should be smoothly feathered.
• *Shoulders:* high, with symmetrical frills.
• *Body:* rounded, semierect.
• *Tail:* narrow and pointed straight down, preferably close to the perch, but not against it or under it.
• *Position:* generally following a figure 7.
• *Legs:* long and stiff, stretched out.
• *Plumage:* sparse, with some frills on shoulders, flanks, and breast; thighs and breast are naked.
• *Length:* 6¼ to 6½ inches (16–17 cm), preferably smaller.

The Gloucester Canary: This "recent" addition to the posture canaries was bred by Mrs. Rogerson from Cheltenham in 1925. The variety came

Some canary breeds: Gloucester (top); border (center); and Norwich (bottom).

about through a cross between the Norwich and the border, the progeny of which were selected for their "small-size" factor, and bred together. There are two types: the Gloucester corona with a crest (crown) and the plain-headed Gloucester consort. Both bird varieties need to be used in breeding, as crest × crest produces a 25% lethal factor.

Characteristics:
• *Corona (crest):* round and symmetrical with the center point coinciding with the center point of the head. Crown should have no interruptions and radiate evenly; it must not cover the eyes.
• *Consort (uncrested):* head should not be too small; bird should reveal light brows.
• *Legs and feet:* medium in length.
• *Body:* well rounded and filled, but somewhat short and stocky.
• *Length:* about 4½ inches (11½ cm) is seen as the ideal length.
• *Position:* active and lively, semierect and proud.
• *Plumage:* smooth and well closed.
• *Condition:* lively, healthy, smooth feathering.

Selected Popular Pet Birds

The Lancashire Canary: This breed, established as far back as the 1820s or 30s, is the largest—8 inches (20 cm)—posture canary. The crest is horseshoe in shape with the feathers flowing forward and outward over the beak and eyes with perfect radiation. At the back of the head the feathers lie flat so as to merge imperceptibly with the neck feathers. The Second World War caused the bird to disappear almost completely, and the few birds we see today are mainly reconstructed from Yorkshire and crested canaries. The Lancashire exists in the two forms usual for all crested canaries; the terms "coppy" and "plainhead" are applied to correspond to "crest" and "crest-bred" (see page 95). It is immaterial which sex carries the crest when pairing crest to crest-bred (coppy to plainhead).

The Official Standard consists of a written description:

"The Lancashire should be a large bird, of good length and stoutness, and when in the show cage should have a bold look. The coppy should be of a horseshoe shape, commencing behind the eye line, and lay close behind the skull, forming a frontal three-quarters of a circle without any break in its shape or formation, and should radiate from its center with a slight droop. There should be no roughness at the back of the skull. The neck should be long and thick, and the feathers lying soft and close; the shoulders broad, the back long and full, and the chest bold and wide. The wings of the Lancashire should be long, giving the bird what is called a long-sided appearance. The tail should also be long. When placed in a show cage, the bird should stand erect, easy and graceful, being bold in its appearance, and not timid or crouching. It should not be dull or slothful looking, and should move about with ease and elegance. Its legs should be long and in strength match the appearance of the body. When standing upright in the cage, the tail should droop slightly, giving the bird the appearance of having a slight curve from the beak to the end of the tail. A Lancashire should neither stand across the perch nor show a hollow back. It should have plenty of feathers lying closely to the body and the feathers should be fine and soft. The properties of the plainhead are the same as the coppy, with the exception of the head. The head should be broad and rather long, the eyebrows clearly defined and overhanging or what is called lashed. The feathers on the head should be soft and plentiful, and not look tucked or whipped up from behind the eye into the neck. The aim in breeding should be to keep and improve the size and length of the bird, at the same time losing nothing of its gracefulness, its beauty of feather, and general contour."

The Lizard Canary: Toward the end of the sixteenth century, the Huguenots fled to England and brought their pets along with them, among which was their type of canary. The lizard completed its development in England, although this variety, which is undoubtedly one of the oldest posture canaries that we know today, did not undergo many changes in its first four-hundred years.

Their so-called sprangling (a series of black crescent-shaped spots running down the back and sides of the bird in orderly parallel rows and extending well across the back from shoulder to shoulder) set them apart from other canary varieties, and are reminiscent of the scales of a lizard, which is obviously how these birds got their name. The lizard's clear head feathers form what is known as the "cap." This cap should be of even size, nicely oval, and should extend from the beak to the base of the skull. The cap should not encroach upon the face of the canary, as this is a fault known as "baldface." It is also a fault if the cap extends down the neck.

If a cap is broken by dark feathers—*not* a fault!—it is known as a "broken cap," and if the whole cap is obliterated by dark feathers, it is called a "noncap." Show classes for "clear cap," "broken cap," and "noncap" are for birds of any age.

Special terms are used when talking about this beautiful and popular variety:

- *Cloudy:* spangling that is not clearly defined.
- *Eyelash:* a line of dark feathers over the eye which

improves the finish of the cap.
- *Grizzled:* a grayish tint in the plumage.
- *Lacing:* color edging on wing butts and coverts.
- *Lineage:* straight rows of spangling.
- *Mooning:* another term for spangling.
- *Muddy:* another term for cloudy.
- *Rowing:* markings of breast and flanks. These must be clear, distinct, and in lines.
- *Star shoulder:* the presence of white feathers in the wing butts.
- *Work:* The profusion of markings.

From the above we can conclude that the lizard canary may well be a color or color-marked variety. According to the Confederation Ornithologique Mondiale (C.O.M.), it is at least partially a posture canary, and this was maintained at the congress in Munich, Germany, in 1972; seeing the characteristic breast, the position, and the size of the lizard, this certainly seems to be a valid viewpoint!

Characteristics:
- *Ground color:* yellow-white or red factor.
- *Cap:* same as ground color, so yellow-white or red factor.
- *Spangling:* the "scale" markings can be black, agate or brown; the same applies to the rowings—the markings on the underside of the body.
- *Type of coloring:* intensive or frosted.
- *Back markings:* should be regular and even, starting at the neck and becoming larger on the back.
- *Plumage:* smooth and well closed, giving a silky impression.

The Northern Dutch Frill: The origin of the Northern or North Dutch frill is rather obscure. According to various experts there is, however, a definite possibility that the first frilled canaries came from the Netherlands around the end of the eighteenth or beginning of the nineteenth century. The first Dutch interests were concentrated in the area of selecting long-feathered canaries. "Through these long feathers," according to Mr. M. Legendre, an important member of the C.O.I., "which originally were concentrated mostly on the breast and

soon started to fall somewhat open, a comparison to Dutch national dress was obvious. From the drawings we were given to examine, the feathering on the back and flanks also became thicker, not so much in the form of curls but more like a scoop. The breeding of this variety spread to Belgium and then to the northern areas of France, especially Roubaix and even further south to Picardie, where the frill was named Roubaisien and "Picardien." Later he was named the Northern Dutch frill. If we delve further into the history of this frilled variety, we will see that the breeding of this bird went as far south as Paris, where the Parisian frill was then developed."

Characteristics:
- *Head and neck:* small and without frills; slightly raised.
- *Mantle:* without many curled feathers; symmetrical.
- *Breast feathering:* fairly well-developed; symmetrical.
- *Flanks:* curled feathers directed upwards; symmetrical.
- *Legs:* fairly long and slightly bent; thighs should be well covered by feathers.
- *Length:* 6½ inches (17 cm).
- *Position:* proud and fairly upright on the perch at an 85° angle and with a slight bend in its posture.

The Norwich Canary: The birthplace of this variety is somewhere in Flanders, Belgium. From there it was exported to Norwich, England, where it was improved by using the lizard canary, as evidenced by the silky and shiny feathers. This grand but somewhat clumsy bird is known as the "John Bull" of the fancy, due to its stocky build with broad back.

Characteristics:
- *Form:* short, broad head; round, well-filled, short body; well-filled neck; and well-filled and broad breast.
- *Posture:* the head, neck, body, and tail should follow a smooth line that parallels a 45° angle. The legs are short.
- *Length:* 6¼ to 6½ inches (16–17 cm)—preferably

6¼ inches (16 cm).

• *Wings:* well closed and short; the tips should be touching and should cover the root of the tail.
• *Feathering:* silky and close.
• *Tail:* closed, short, and held straight.
• *Condition:* healthy and relaxed in movement.

The Parisian Frill Canary: In this variety there lurk some real giants of the canary world, some of which have tail feathers that alone measure 4¾ inches (12 cm)! It would seem obvious that they have not always been this large—I saw some birds in Brazil and Spain that exceeded 9 inches (22 cm)!—but we know very little about the origin of this variety, though many experts think that the Northern Dutch frill (see page 98) should be considered the "forefather." The Parisian frill completed its development in Paris and surrounding areas, and in 1867 an organization already existed honoring this variety. This lovely bird is certainly deserving of the attention, with its robust build, proud posture, and the symmetry of its tightly curled frills. The better these three points, the higher a score a Parisian frill will be able to claim at a show.

Characteristics:
• *Length:* 8 to 9 inches (20–22 cm); circumference of the feathering: 11 to 24¼ inches (28–62 cm).
• *Position:* semierect, proud and brave.
• *Plumage:* evenly distributed frills, which should be fine.
• *Mantle:* abundant and well-developed shoulder and back frills.
• *Breast*: well fitted with symmetrical breast frills.
• *Flanks:* symmetrical with mantle and breast feathers.
• *Tail frills:* these are located at the root of the tail, should be olive-shaped, and look something like rooster feathers. They should be long and full and fall evenly from the rump.
• *Head and neck feathers:* there are two possibilities here—either "casquette" type where the curled feathers form a perfect transition to the smooth head, or "calotte" type where the feathers make a curly transition to a frilled head.

• *Legs and feet:* should be well developed; the toenails may grow in the shape of a corkscrew.
• *Tail:* closed, long, and broad; a swallow's tail or indented bottom edge is considered a serious fault.
• *Wings:* well closed and long.
• *Condition:* healthy, proud, and very clean.

The Scotch Fancy Canary: The origin of the Scotch fancy is not entirely clear, but it is presumed that it evolved from the Belgian bult and another variety which will probably always remain a mystery. There have been some educated guesses made, such as the Southern Dutch frill, but the Scotch fancy has a definite "hump" which it inherited from the bossu; I find it rather doubtful that the Southern Dutch frill would have already been known in Scotland during those years. As you can see, there are still plenty of questions!

Characteristics:
• *Form:* shape of a half moon, with high shoulders without giving a "saddle" impression.
• *Head and neck:* fine and narrow; the neck should be thin and long, but gradually becoming thicker and fuller at the shoulders.
• *Shoulders:* round and narrow but well proportioned.
• *Back:* round and long, but well filled.
• *Tail:* long, small, and fine, with the point sticking out at an angle under the perch.
• *Position:* the bird should be standing high on its legs, with toes steadily grasping the perch. The body itself is in a semicircular posture. The bird is very active, howerer, and will not stand still easily.
• *Length:* 6¼ to 6½ inches (16–17 cm), preferably larger.
• *Condition:* as healthy and pure as possible, without any damaged feathers or legs.

The Southern Dutch Frill Canary: Although the name would not give it away, this frill canary really originated in Italy, specifically from around Naples, Vaserte, Benevente, and southern Italy. This variety probably inherited the high back from the Belgian bult and the frill from the Northern Dutch frill (see page 98). It is also presumed that the

Southern or South Dutch frill contributed to the development of the gibber italicus (see page 96). As far as can be determined, the Southern Dutch frill first appeared after the First World War, and about 20 years later reached its peak. The bird was fairly well proportioned, the shape of a figure 7 was practically perfected, and the shape of the head was much like that of a lizard. When the bird sits on the perch, its legs are stretched out and its tail almost touches the perch. A characteristic of this variety is that they are very nervous, which can be seen during exhibitions, with the bird moving from side to side and regularly holding onto the front of the cage with one foot. This is why the scale of points allows for such behavior, since it is so typical. It is unfortunate that this bird has become quite rare and that the breeding material that is still available is rather heavily inbred, so degeneration is anything but imaginary. If there were some good breeding material available, this interesting frill would certainly be able to capture more fans.

Characteristics:

• *Head and neck:* small head, like a lizard; small beak. Neck is elongated and "snaky" in appearance.

• *Position:* ideally a figure 7. Head and neck should stick out. The wings should be somewhat erect. Tail bends inward a little, almost touching the perch. Thighs should be well covered with feathering. Feet are stretched out.

• *Body:* well rounded and long.

• *Length:* 6¼ to 6½ inches (16–17 cm).

• *Mantle:* symmetrical frills; regular and full.

• *Breast feathers:* curling toward each other from left to right, and symmetrical (jabots). The frills give the impression that they form a little basket.

• *Flanks:* these feathers should curl upward and be equally long on both flanks; they should also be symmetrical and full.

• *Tail:* long and especially well closed; as mentioned, slightly bent inward, almost touching the tail.

• *Wings:* well closed, but the tips must not overlap.

• *Plumage:* undamaged and soft.

• *Condition:* brisk, proud, and healthy.

The Yorkshire Canary: This "gentleman of the fancy" first appeared in Yorkshire, England, around 1870, and especially in Bradford. In 1894, the first official standard was drawn up; in the late 1920s and early 1930s the breed reached the peak of its development. Before the turn of the century, however, it was desirable that this bird be able "to pass through the wedding band of a canary fancier." The variety is currently a great deal larger!

Characteristics:

• *Head and neck:* full, round head; the skull must definitely not be flat, perferably somewhat on the broad side. Short, thick, well-filled neck.

• *Body:* well rounded and gradually tapering; "invisible" shoulders; nicely rounded breast and back.

• *Tail:* in one line with the back; closed and straight.

• *Position:* proud and erect.

• *Length:* 6½ to 8 inches (17–20 cm)—no larger, no smaller.

• *Plumage:* short, closed, and tight. Well-closed wings.

• *Color:* as pure as possible, preferably one color, although pied is permissible.

• *Condition:* a generally healthy impression; lively nature.

Budgerigars or Parakeets

The budgerigar was first brought to Europe from Australia in the nineteenth century and is today one of the most popular of all cage birds. As soon as it was discovered that other color varieties could be developed from the original grass green by selective breeding, the popularity of these birds increased tremendously. The yellow variety was the least difficult to produce, as these occur even in wild populations, and some of these were brought to Europe around 1850 and further propagated. But it

Selected Popular Pet Birds

Stackable breeding cages for parakeets, lovebirds, finches, or canaries.

was a sensation when news came from Belgium and, shortly after, France in 1890 that a blue budgie had been bred. A third color variety is the white, which was parented by a green pair of which the grandparents were born from blue and yellow birds. These white birds had dark eyes and, in fact, were not pure white, as when viewed in a certain light, the green coloration of the parent birds was still visible. The albino variety is, however, pure white, but always with red eyes. Next, there is a yellow bird with red eyes which is called a lutino and which is regarded as an albino variety of the green and yellow color forms, while the white with red eyes is the albino of the blue color form. Lutino and albino varieties are not old; the first albino appeared in Germany in 1932. With green birds we have light greens and olive greens; while with the blues, we have light blue, cobalt blue, and mauve. With the normal yellow, we can distinguish light yellow, dark yellow and olive yellow. Moreover, for some time we have known of blue budgies with the white of the face replaced by yellow; green budgies with

yellow wings; blue budgies with white wings; cinnamon-and cobalt-colored birds, and birds of whom half the body is mauve and the other half olive green. More recent varieties, such as the opalines, fallows, spangleds, and other colors, testify to man's enthusiasm in producing new color varieties.

The parakeet is an easy bird to keep. It will thrive on the various food mixtures (see page 46) you can obtain in the shops—especially if these are complemented with a regular supply of unripe weed seeds, as well as seeding grasses, which in its native land of Australia are its favorite food. A couple of leafy twigs, such as those of the willow, from which it can tear off the bark and leaves, will be gratefully accepted and will be a welcome part of its diet. Green food, such as carrots, lettuce, and similar greens (see page 53), will be taken eagerly; most birds will also appreciate a little apple, pear, or other fruit (see page 52). The budgerigar drinks sparingly, especially from a fountain. In the arid lands of its natural habitat, the budgie often slakes its thirst by drinking the dewdrops that hang on the grass; if you spray the cage on warm summer days with a mist sprayer, ensure that you leave drops hanging on the mesh. These will be eagerly sucked up. The budgie does not bathe very often if at all, although there are some that will get a sudden idea to try it out and thereafter are difficult to stop. In the outside aviary, budgies should be protected from excessive rain, preferably by covering part of the roof with transparent, plastic sheeting. Although it quickly acclimates to the cold winter weather, you should ensure that it has a frost-free shelter in which to spend the night.

The budgerigar will breed readily in nest boxes from poplar or birch wood of the type to be found in most pet shops or avicultural suppliers and, providing you follow a few simple rules, the birds will breed year round. It is best, however—especially in outdoor aviaries—to remove the nest boxes in August to prevent the birds' attempting to rear chicks during the colder months of the year. The boxes can then be replaced in the spring for a new breeding season. The clutch usually consists of three to five eggs, but it is not unusual for a hen to lay ten eggs in as little as ten days.

Parrots and Parrotlike Birds

Parrots are regarded as the "monkeys" among the birds, through the fact that they climb well, and use their beaks as a "third leg." They can hang upside-down from a branch without falling, as their feet are used as "hands." You have probably seen a parrot eating a peanut from its "fist."

In the wild, parrotlike birds can pluck various fruits with their feet and bring them to the beak to eat. The fact that they have two toes pointing forward and two pointing backwards (a so-called zygodactyl foot, which they share with woodpeckers and cuckoos) makes their feet excellent tools for climbing and for holding large chunks of food. Parrots and flamingos have an upper mandible that is hinged to the skull and that may be moved freely. In parrots, the beak is a very special tool. They use it for climbing and for opening particularly hard fruits and seeds; they use it for gnawing wood, especially in the construction of their nest cavities—perhaps to make the entrance hole wider, or the cavity deeper. You probably know all about their habit of chewing up perches and nest boxes.

Most parrot varieties breed in tree hollows. They rarely use nest material, but commonly enlarge the nest hollow. The eggs are then laid on the bare timber. Some species use a little nest material in the form of peat dust, mold, twigs, and leaves as a "lining." The lovebird species takes this a stage further—they construct a nest inside the cavity from grass and fibers, but especially from twigs which they cut into lengths and transport to the nest box tucked into their rump and back feathers. One species, the Quaker or monk parakeet (*Myiopsitta monachus*) from South America, really builds a

large nest with an entrance hole in the side. Sometimes several pairs build in the same nest complex, each pair having its own chamber under the same roof.

The incubation period of parrots ranges from 18 days for the smaller grass parakeets to 30 for the larger species such as African gray parrots. In nearly all species, the hen broods alone; the cock feeds her during this time, however. Exceptions are the cockatoos and cockatiels, where the cock also takes his turn at brooding. The young take rather a long time to fledge; with smaller parakeets it may take five to seven weeks; with larger parrots six weeks or more.

Parrotlike birds feed on ripe and unripe seeds, green food, buds, bark, and various fruits (see page 47). Their diet must be as varied as possible. During the rearing of chicks they must have access to various half-ripe seeds, sprouting millet and oats, and as much green food as possible. Some breeders recommend egg food, hard-boiled egg, and ant pupae as supplements. In addition, various twigs are valuable to alleviate boredom.

Parrotlike Birds

Monk Parakeet (*Myiopsitta monachus*): *Size:* 12 inches (30 cm). *Distribution:* Southern Brazil to central Argentina; introduced into New York, New Jersey, Connecticut, Massachusetts, Virginia, and Florida. *Clutch:* 4–8 eggs. *Incubation:* 26–28 days. *Fledging:* 42–44 days. The female builds the bullet-shaped nest and cleans and extends it each year; the nest consists of two "rooms." The eggs are hatched in the "back room," while the room that leads to the "portico" could be considered a "living room," since the parents spend most of their time here, including the night. When the young are bigger, they too will move into the "living room." This permits the female to start a new clutch in the back "room." Breeding box: $6 \times 12 \times 17\frac{1}{2}$ inches ($15 \times 30 \times 45$ cm); entrance: 3 inches (8 cm).

Green-rumped Parrotlet (*Forpus passer-*

Selected Popular Pet Birds

inus): *Size:* 4¾ inches (12 cm). *Distribution:* Guyana, Surinam, Venezuela, Trinidad, and Colombia. *Clutch:* 4–5 white eggs, sometimes as many as 7, deposited on alternate days. *Incubation:* 21–23 days. Only the female sits on the eggs; the male, however, feeds her and later the young. *Fledging:* 30–35 days. The young are fed by both parents for at least another 14 days. Separate the fledglings from the parents once they have become independent. This procedure will allow and encourage the female to start on the next brood. There is room for three broods per year, but not more. Nest box: 5 × 5 × 8 inches (13 × 13 × 20 cm); entrance 1½ inches (4 cm).

Pacific or Celestial Parrotlet (*Forpus coelestis*): *Size:* 4¾ inches (12 cm). *Distribution:* Tropical areas of western South America. *Clutch:* 4–5 white eggs, sometimes 6. *Incubation:* 20–22 days. Only the female sits on the eggs. *Fledging:* 30–34 days. Newly imported and breeding birds often attack each other's legs and feet. Two to three broods per year are possible, even when housed in a large cage. Cover the bottom of the nest box with a thick layer (1 inch [2½ cm]) of wood shavings and moss. For more details see green-rumped parrotlet.

Peach-fronted Conure (*Aratinga aurea*): *Size:* 11 inches (28 cm). *Distribution:* Brazil. *Clutch:* 2 white eggs. *Incubation:* 30–32 days; both sexes sit on the eggs. *Fledging:* After approximately 50 days. It is advisable to remove fellow species from the aviary, because the male will very actively defend his young. Nest box: 14 × 10 × 10 inches (35 × 25 × 25 cm); entrance : 3 inches (8 cm). The menu of the majority of the Aratinga species should consist of grass seeds, hemp, oats, fruits, fresh buds, boiled or soaked seeds, corn, soaked white bread, live food (mealworms, white worms, "ant-eggs," etc.), nuts, berries, hard-boiled eggs, etc.

Brown-throated Conure (*Aratinga pertinax*): *Size:* 12 inches (30 cm). *Distribution:* Curaçao and St. Thomas. *Clutch:* 2–3 white eggs. *Incubation:* 26–30 days. *Fledging:* After approximately 48–50 days. Nest box: 12 × 12 × 14 inches (30 × 30 × 35 cm);

Left to right: pennant rosella, monk parakeet and golden–fronted parakeet.

entrance: 3 inches (8 cm). The female is a little smaller, and her coloring is somewhat duller. This species will not breed easily in captivity. All Aratinga species have a sharp and raucous voice, and are often very destructive.

Red-fronted Conure (*Aratinga wagleri frontata*): *Size:* 14½ inches (37 cm). *Distribution:* Ecuador and western Peru. *Clutch:* 3–4 white eggs. *Incubation:* 30 days. *Fledging:* Approximately 40 days. The adult female is somewhat smaller and the red on her wings is often duller. As far as I know no breeding results have been achieved in captivity. My wife had a red-fronted conure during her youth who could quote a few lines of Keats' work "Endymion": "A thing of beauty is a joy forever/Its loveliness increases/it will never pass into nothingness." This bird attracted quite some interest in Tampa, Florida, and was so tame that she would accompany my wife on her shoulder on the way to college. Then the bird remained in the trees by the school until my wife returned to pick her up again.

Cactus Conure (*Aratinga actorum*): *Size:* 10 inches (25 cm). *Distribution:* Brazil. *Clutch:* 3–4 white eggs. *Incubation:* 28–30 days. *Fledging:* Approximately 40 days. This species is quite suitable for either a roomy cage or an aviary. In the wild this species lives primarily on cactus seeds—hence its name—as well as on fruits and berries. I believe this is one of the most affectionate pets you can have in your home!

Jendaya Conure (*Aratinga jandaya*): *Size:* 12 inches (30 cm). *Distribution:* Northeastern Brazil. *Clutch:* 3–4 white eggs. *Incubation:* 26 days; incubated by both sexes. *Fledging:* 55–57 days. Cover the bottom of the nest box (10 × 10 × 14 inches [25 × 25 × 35 cm]; entrance: 3 inches [8 cm]) with a thick layer of small twigs and peat moss. For extra nutritional benefits, supply these noisy, nervous, but colorful birds with fresh twigs and branches (willow, fruit trees, etc.); different kinds of fruits (coconut, cherries, apple, banana, berries); nuts and corn. The fresh twigs are important because these birds have an enormous gnawing instinct: virtually nothing is safe from them!

Nanday Conure (*Nandayus nenday*): *Size:* 12 inches (30 cm). *Distribution:* Southeastern Bolivia, southern Mato Grosso, Brazil, Paraguay, and northern Argentina. *Clutch:* 2–5 white eggs. *Incubation:* 25 days; incubated only by the female. *Fledging:* 50–55 days. Nest box: 12 × 12 × 14 inches (30 × 30 × 35 cm); entrance: 3 inches (8 cm). These species are pleasant to keep, although they do have one drawback: They have a long, raucous call to which they give voice with and without provocation—they are much too loud to keep indoors. They can be tamed very quickly and will take treats out of their keeper's hand in no time at all; they are also good talkers, although their vocabulary will never be more than limited.

Maroon-bellied Conure (*Pyrrhura frontalis*): *Size:* 9 inches (23 cm). *Distribution:* Southeastern

Top: nandaya (left) and cactus conure (right). Bottom: white–eared conure.

Brazil. *Clutch:* 4–6 white eggs. *Incubation:* 26–28 days; incubated only by the female. *Fledging:* 45–50 days. Nest box: 10 × 10 × 14 inches (25 × 25 × 35 cm); entrance: 3 inches (8 cm). The best breeding results are achieved if a pair is kept in a garden aviary without any other birds. Imported birds are restless, somewhat wild, and constantly flying against the bars or mesh. To avoid injuries attach various natural branches to the mesh.

White-eared Conure (*Pyrrhura leucotis*): *Size:* 9 inches (23 cm). *Distribution:* Coastal states of Brazil and northern Venezuela. *Clutch:* 5–9 white eggs. *Incubation:* 22–25 days; incubated only by the female. *Fledging:* 35–38 days. A nesting box, possibly of beech, 10 × 10 × 14 inches (25 × 25 × 35 cm), with an opening 3 inches (8 cm), is recommended (also for the maroon-bellied conure!). Young birds must have soaked white bread, some sunflower seeds, hemp and oats, and cooked corn as a daily supplement, as well as carrot strips, fresh twigs, and leaf buds.

Barred, Catherine, or Lineolated Parakeet (*Bolborhynchus lineola*): *Size:* 6¾ inches (17 cm). *Distribution:* Central America, from Mexico to Panama. *Clutch:* 4–5 white eggs. *Incubation:* 22–23 days; incubated only by the female. *Fledging:* 38–40 days. This is an excellent species for an outdoor community aviary. The bird is particularly fond of various types of fruits and berries, canary-grass seeds, fresh twigs, buds, and small insects. In regard to the latter, it is an excellent idea to rake the ground of the aviary deeply a few times each week. Nest box: 6 × 6 × 12 inches (15 × 15 × 30 cm); entrance: 3 inches (8 cm). Outside the breeding season the nest box will also be used as sleeping quarters.

Golden-fronted Parakeet (*Bolborhynchus aurifrons*): *Size:* 6¾ inches (17 cm). *Distribution:* Peru, Bolivia, Chile, and Argentina. *Clutch:* 3–4 white eggs. *Incubation:* 23 days. *Fledging:* 35–38 days. The nest box must be placed horizontally: 6 × 6 × 10 inches (15 × 15 × 25 cm), with a 31½-inch- (80 cm) deep tunnel-type entrance; entrance: 3-inch (8 cm) diameter; the box itself should have two chambers: a small opening (diameter 3 inches [8 cm]) connects both chambers. One of the chambers will be used as a "maternity room"; the other as sleeping quarters.

Orange-chinned Parakeet (*Brotogeris jugularis*): *Size:* 8 inches (20 cm). *Distribution:* Southern Mexico to Colombia. *Clutch:* 2–6 white eggs. *Incubation:* 60 days. *Fledging:* 35 days. Nest box: 8 × 8 × 10 inches (20 × 20 × 25 cm); entrance: 2⅜ inches (6 cm), or a 25-gallon drum filled with moistened moss which is then left to dry. The birds will carve their nest in this moss; in the wild they sometimes use a termite's nest. The young are reared on a diet of soft leaf buds, twigs, fruits, insects, and seeds. The nest box is usually used as sleeping quarters.

Tui Parakeet (*Brotogeris santithomae*): *Size:*

7¼ inches (18½ cm). *Distribution:* Western Brazil, Peru, lower Amazon, and Ecuador. *Clutch:* 4–5 white eggs. *Incubation:* 20–21 days. *Fledging:* 60 days. The daily diet of the *Brotogeris* species should consist of cherries, apples, pears, bananas, pineapples (in pieces), soaked raisins and currants, corn, rice, oats, fresh buds, various grasses, occasionally hemp, millet spray, and small insects (beetles, white worms). In the wild these birds sometimes make their nest in termite hills. A roomy beechwood nesting box (8 × 8 × 10 inches [20 × 20 × 25 cm]); entrance: 2⅜ inches [6 cm]) is often used as sleeping quarters.

Canary-winged Parakeet (*Brotogeris versicolor chiriri*): *Size:* 10 inches (25 cm). *Distribution:* Bolivia, eastern and central Brazil, and eastern Peru. *Clutch:* 3–5 white eggs. *Incubation:* 26 days. *Fledging:* Approximately 60 days. The bottom of the beechwood nest box should be covered with a layer of moist peat moss about 1½ inches (4 cm) thick. Nest box: see orange-chinned parakeet.

Gray-cheeked Parakeet (*Brotogeris pyrrhopterus*): *Size:* 8¼ inches (21 cm). *Distribution:* Northwestern Peru and western Ecuador. *Clutch:* 4–6 white eggs. *Incubation:* 22 days. Only the female incubates the eggs, while the male guards the nest from a nearby post. *Fledging:* 60 days. Nest box: see orange-chinned parakeet. The bottom should be covered with a thick layer of moss or peat moss (3 inches [8 cm]).

Ringneck Parakeet (*Psittacula krameri manillensis*): *Size:* 16 inches (41 cm). *Distribution:* India, Pakistan, Nepal, and Sri Lanka; introduced to Singapore. *Clutch:* 3–5 white eggs. *Incubation:* 22–26 days. *Fledging:* 50–52 days. These birds are ideal as aviary pets because they will breed easily. They should be housed in an aviary of generous proportions, at least 12 to 16 feet long (4–5 m), because it has happened more than once that males housed in small areas became sterile. Well-known mutations are lutino, blue, albino, cinnamon, and gray.

Red-rumped Parakeet (*Psephotus*

Selected Popular Pet Birds

haematonotus): *Size:* 10 to 11 inches (25–28 cm). *Distribution:* Southeastern Australia. *Clutch:* 4–7 white eggs. *Incubation:* 19 days. *Fledging:* 30–33 days. Once independent, young birds should be separated from the parents because the male will chase and possibly injure them.

Western or Stanley Rosella (*Platycercus*

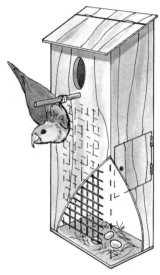

The grandfather clock nest box for a gray–cheeked parakeet. Note the cutaway section in the drawing to show the wire against the inside front of the nest box, for obvious reasons.

icterotis): *Size:* 11–12 inches, (26–28 cm). *Distribution:* Southwestern Australia. *Clutch:* 4–6 eggs. *Incubation:* 19–21 days. *Fledging:* 30–33 days. Couples like to have a roomy aviary to themselves—like all rosella species! Their song is quite pleasant. Nest box: 9 × 9 × 24 inches (23 × 23 × 60 cm); Entrance: 2⅜ inches (6 cm).

Crimson Rosella or Pennant (*Platycercus elegans*): *Size:* 12½ to 14 inches (32–36 cm). *Distribution:* East and southeastern Australia; intro-

duced into New Zealand and Norfolk Island. *Clutch:* 4–8 eggs. *Incubation:* 21 days. *Fledging:* 34–36 days. Their song is a little shrill, but not altogether unpleasant, since it does include some musical notes. A noteworthy fact about their song is that it is imitated by the lyre bird.

Bourke's Parrot (*Neophema bourkii*): *Size:* 8⅝ inches (22 cm). *Distribution:* Australia. *Clutch:* 4–7 white eggs. *Incubation:* 18 days; incubated by the female. *Fledging:* 28–30 days. Bourke's parrots make reliable foster parents for both their own fellows and species belonging to the genus *Psephotus*. Nest box: 18 × 6 × 6 inches (45 × 15 × 15 cm); entrance: 2⅜ inches (6 cm). Young birds that are leaving the nest are quite wild. Keep a close watch on them because they may very well injure themselves flying against the walls and mesh; sticking some green twigs through the mesh of roof and sides will alert them to the obstacles. The young are reared by the male on canary-rearing food, ant eggs, soaked rice, corn, bread soaked in milk, and various seeds (canary-grass seed, panicum millet, oats, hemp, weed and grass seeds, etc.). When the birds are given good care, owners have little trouble in keeping them healthy and lively, and encouraging them to breed.

Turquoise Parrot (*Neophema pulchella*): *Size:* 8½ inches (21 cm). *Distribution:* Queensland, Australia. *Clutch:* 4–5, sometimes 8 white eggs. *Incubation:* 19–20 days. *Fledging:* 32 days. This species is not tolerant toward other Neophema species. Nest box: 8 × 16 × 8 inches (20 × 40 × 20 cm); entrance 2⅜ inches (6 cm). Two clutches per year is not at all unusual; in the wild they usually breed three times. The aviary must be roomy and absolutely not damp, because dampness is very dangerous for these active, beautiful birds. The fledglings become independent after two weeks. Young males and females should be separated from their parents, though aggressive pursuit by the father is directed only at the young males. Since the young birds are quite wild and nervous, it is important to place live branches and twigs in the mesh of the roof and sides

Selected Popular Pet Birds

Fischer's lovebird. Bottom: peach–faced lovebird (left) and masked lovebird (right).

the opportunity to see everything that is happening around him or her, you should experience little trouble with deserted nests.

Fischer's Lovebird (*Agapornis personata fischeri*): *Size:* 4 inches (10 cm). *Distribution:* Africa, south and southeast of Lake Victoria. *Clutch:* 4–6 white eggs. *Incubation:* 20–25 days. *Fledging:* 35–37 days. As soon as the chicks are independent—usually 10–12 days after fledging—it is best to separate them from their parents. In 1979, a blue mutation was bred in California.

Masked Lovebird (*Agapornis personata personata*): *Size:* 6 inches (15 cm). *Distribution:* Africa, northern Tanzania. *Clutch:* 3–5 eggs. *Incubation:* 21–23 days. *Fledging:* 44–46 days. A wild-caught blue mutant is now an often-bred color and commonly available; the wild form, however, has become extremely scarce.

Peach-faced Lovebird (*Agapornis roseicollis*): *Size:* 6½ to 7 inches (16–18 cm). *Dis-*

of the aviary to help warn the young of the obstacles in their new environment.

Cockatiel (*Nymphicus hollandicus*): *Size:* 12–14 inches (30–35 cm). *Distribution:* Central Australia; introduced to Tasmania. *Clutch:* 4–8 white eggs. *Incubation:* 18–21 days; the hen incubates the eggs during the night, and the male during the day. *Fledging:* 30–35 days. Always form pairs by placing an inexperienced bird with a bird that knows its way around and has already raised a family. Nest box 13 × 8 × 18 inches (35 × 20 × 45 cm), and an entrance hole 2⅜ inches (6 cm). The young, which initially resemble the female, often stick their little heads out of the nest opening, making a peeping and hissing noise. It is advisable to make the nest box so the bird on the eggs will have its head at the height of the entrance; therefore don't make the opening too high up. You should place a thick layer of sawdust or peat moss on the bottom. Don't use a nest box where the entrance is too low, either, because cockatiels have the habit of leaving the nest when they are startled. When the bird on the nest has

A lovebird nest box, with a perforated zinc bottom, placed over a tray with water. Water vapor can pass through the perforation and thus keep the shell membrane of the egg moist and supple enough.

tribution: Southwestern parts of Africa. *Clutch:* 4–5 white eggs. *Incubation:* 22–23 days. After the second egg, the hen begins to incubate. *Fledging:* 30–35 days. Independent young should be housed in a separate, roomy pen. No more than three clutches per breeding season are allowed. This species is supposedly the first member of its genus to have been seen transporting nest-building material between its back and rump feathers. A large number of color mutations are now being bred, especially in the United States and Europe (Holland, Belgium, Denmark, Germany, and England); well-known mutations are pied, dark factor, yellow, lutino, and pastel blue—one of the "oldest" mutations, first appearing in the Netherlands in 1963.

Leadbeater's Cockatoo (*Cacatua leadbeateri*): *Size:* 13½ inches (34 cm). *Distribution:* Australia, except in the farthest southwest. *Clutch:* 2–5 white eggs. *Incubation:* 28–30 days. During the day the female broods, in the late evening and night the male incubates. *Fledging:* 8–9 weeks. Good results can be expected when the birds have a partly decayed tree trunk with an opening about 34 inches (87 cm) deep, with a diameter of 10 inches (5 cm).

Moluccan Cockatoo (*Cacatua moluccensis*): *Size:* 20 inches (52 cm). *Distribution:* Southern Moluccas, Ceram, Sapurua, Haruko; introduced into Amboina. *Clutch:* 1–2 white eggs. Incubation: 28–35 days. *Fledging:* 14–15 weeks. These noisy birds grow tame and affectionate in no time at all, especially toward children.

Umbrella Cockatoo (*Cacatua alba*): *Size:* 18 inches (46 cm). *Distribution:* North and South Moluccas. *Clutch:* 1–2 white eggs. *Incubation:* 25–27 days. *Fledging:* 16–18 weeks. These destructive and noisy but beautiful birds require a large aviary, and a nest box 19½ × 16½ × 19½ inches (50 × 40 × 50 cm). This bird is no great talker, but exceptionally gentle and very easy to tame.

Lesser Sulphur-crested Cockatoo (*Cacatua sulphurea*): *Size:* 12 inches (30 cm). *Distribution:*

Top: Moluccan cockatoo (left) and Leadbeater's cockatoo (right). Bottom: Galah cockatoo (left) and lesser sulphur–crested cockatoo (right).

Indonesia and Celebes in various subspecies. *Clutch:* 2–3 white eggs. *Incubation:* 27–28 days by both sexes: the male incubates during the day, the female during the night (the reverse of most cockatoo species!). *Fledging:* 10–12 weeks. In captivity, once acclimated, these hardy birds breed regularly, especially when the pair has been together for a few years. Psittacine beak and feather disease (PBFD; see page 85) in young adults is especially prevalent in this species.

Greater Sulphur-crested Cockatoo (*Cacatua galerita*): *Size:* 20 inches (50 cm). *Distribution:* Northern, eastern, and southern Australia, New Guinea, and Melanesia, in various species. Introduced into New Zealand. *Clutch:* 2 white eggs. *Incubation:* 28–30 days. *Fledging:* 6–8 weeks. This species is by far one of the most popular of all cockatoos as a pet, notwithstanding its propensity to shriek at inopportune moments. The bird, Cocky, a resident of the London Zoological Gardens, died at an authenticated age of 142 years!

Galah or Rose-breasted Cockatoo (*Eolophus roseicapillus*): *Size:* 13½ inches (35 cm). *Distribution:* Australia and Tasmania, in various subspecies. *Clutch:* 2–5 white eggs. *Incubation:* 24–26 days. *Fledging:* 9–10 weeks; after fledging the young receive the care of both parents for another month. In order to get proper breeding results, moisten the nest box regularly. Use boxes 20 × 20 × 40 inches (51 × 52 × 101 cm); Mr. W. de Grahl recommends boxes 14 × 14 × 20 inches (35 × 35 × 55 cm), with a nest entrance 3½ inches (9 cm). When large boxes are used, fasten a strip of mesh on the inside in order to make it possible for the birds to leave their "maternity room" easily. Galahs are playful, friendly, and fairly good talkers.

Red Lory (*Eos bornea*): *Size:* 12 inches (30 cm). *Distribution:* Amboina, Ceram, and the Moluccas. *Clutch:* 2 eggs. *Incubation:* 23–25 days. *Fledging:* 12–13 weeks. After the young leave the nest they will be fed by both parents for another 2–3 weeks. Offer a nest box 14 × 14 × 18 inches (35 × 35 × 45 cm), with an entrance 3½ inches (9 cm); situate the box in a high place. These playful birds—like many lories and lorikeets—live in groups, usually high up in the trees, looking for pollen, fruit, and nectar; in captivity, however, they must be kept in pairs, as they are often aggressive toward other hookbills. The bird's tongue has elongated papillae on the tip which become erect when feeding, for "harvesting pollen and pressing it into a form suitable for swallowing." (Forshaw). In captivity, the birds feed on milk- and honey-soaked rusks, pure honey, a good vitamin-mineral preparation, berries, fruits, germinated seeds, and a brand of baby food made of fruits and vegetables. There are also excellent commercial lory foods on the market (ask your pet-store manager). Understandably, during hot days it is better to soak the bread in water than in milk. Food should be offered on a feeder that is approximately 5 feet (152 cm) high, as both lories and lorikeets do

Top: red lory (left) and rainbow lorikeet (right). Bottom: electus parrots (female left, male right).

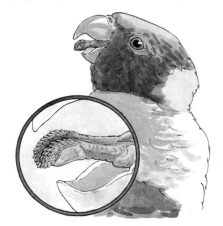

This rainbow lorikeet and all other members of the *Loriidae* group have a "brush tongue." The word "brush" refers to a cluster of elongated papillae, which increase substantially in length when the tongue is protruded.

Selected Popular Pet Birds

Chattering lory, preening. Like most lories and lorikeets, this species prefers to spend the night in a nest box. The male can be hostile toward his young as soon as they have fledged; if this happens the young should be placed in a different run (pen).

not like to forage on the ground.

Rainbow Lorikeet (*Trichoglossus haematodus*): *Size:* 12 inches (30 cm). *Distribution:* Ceram, Moluccas, Amboina, Flores, Bali, Lombok, New Guinea, and eastern Australia, in 21 subspecies. *Clutch:* 2 eggs. *Incubation:* 25–26 days. *Fledging:* 75–80 days. This hardy, active bird breeds frequently. It will eat sunflower seeds, oats, canary-grass seed, spray millet, buckwheat, as well as nectar, pieces of apple, grapes, and carrots fed daily. It is best to keep the birds in pairs in a long aviary with a roomy night shelter; the temperature must be maintained at 75°F (24°C). Nest box: 10 × 10 × 18 inches (25 × 25 × 45 cm); entrance: 3½ inches (9 cm).

Chattering Lory (*Lorius garrulus*): *Size:* 12 inches (30 cm). *Distribution:* Halmahera and several surrounding islands in 3 subspecies. *Clutch:* 2 white eggs. Incubation: 24–26 days. *Fledging:*

10–11 weeks. These lories are easily excited when strangers come near their cage or aviary (they are better suited to aviary life than to being cage birds). They start to screech, are upset for hours, and will even leave their brood unattended for quite some time. The chattering lory must have access to fesh fruits and fruit pulp, and willow branches, chickweed, lettuce, endive, weed seed, honeysticks, spray millet, and cuttlefish bone.

Grand Electus or Electus Parrot (*Electus roratus*): *Size:* 14 inches (35 cm). *Distribution:* Moluccas, Ceram, Amboina, Sumba, Halmahera, Solomon Islands, New Guinea and adjacent islands, and northern Queensland, Australia, in 10 subspecies. *Clutch:* 2 eggs. *Incubation:* 28 days. *Fledging:* 10–11 weeks. As both sexes are totally different in color, it was thought for a very long time that they were two species, until Dr. A. B. Meyer, of the National Museum of Natural History in Munich, Germany, discovered in 1874 that the males are predominantly green and the females red. The female, by the way, often stirs up trouble in the aviary, and may fight for weeks before settling down with her partner. Use a nest box 12 × 12 × 20 inches (30 × 30 × 50 cm), with an entrance 6 inches (15 cm).

Blue and Yellow Macaw (*Ara ararauna*): *Size:* 34 inches (85 cm). *Distribution:* Panama to northern Paraguay. *Clutch:* 2–5 white eggs. *Incubation:* 25–28 days. *Fledging:* After about 3 months. It sometimes takes years before a pair begins to raise a family. Macaws are highly intelligent birds that learn all sorts of tricks, and even a few words in very little time. When properly cared for, they can grow

Above left: The Indian white eye is willing to breed in captivity, but live food is essential throughout the year.
Above right: Dyal thrushes or magpie robins often act aggressively toward smaller birds, but are willing to breed in captivity. Live food is essential.
Below left: Pekin robins like a dry and draft-proof aviary.
Below right: The gold-fronted leafbird is an excellent aviary bird, well known for its beautiful song.

Selected Popular Pet Birds

The blue and yellow macaw prefers using a barrel for a roosting and nesting place; and the same goes for the 14 other species of macaws (*Ara*). All nests should be fixed high in the aviary.

to be very old; one-hundred years and more is not spectacular. Nest box: $20 \times 20 \times 31\frac{1}{2}$ inches ($50 \times 50 \times 80$ cm); entrance: $5\frac{1}{2}$ inches (14 cm).

African Gray Parrot (*Psittacus erithacus*): *Size:* 14 inches (35 cm). *Distribution:* Equatorial Africa, especially in the forests of the Ivory Coast in the west, to the western parts of Kenya in the east, and south as far as the northern parts of Angola, and southern Congo and northwestern Tanzania. The darker-colored subspecies *P.c. timneh* (timneh African gray parrot) is from Guinea, Sierra Leone, Liberia, and the western parts of the Ivory Coast. *Clutch:* 2–3 white eggs. *Incubation:* 29–30 days. *Fledging:* 10–11 weeks. After the young leave the

Above left: The shama thrush or white-rumped shama is best known for its splendid song and mimicry.
Above right: The red-eared bulbul is easy to keep and has a melodious song.
Below: The pagoda mynah is an attractive, hardy avairy bird, but it should not be kept with small softbills

nest they will be fed by their parents for at least another 4 months. For breeding you need a pair that is sexually mature, which means that the birds must be at least 5 to 6 years of age. Nest box: $16 \times 18 \times 26$ inches ($40 \times 45 \times 65$ cm); entrance: 6 inches (15 cm). The African Gray Parrot is an excellent talker and mimic.

Senegal Parrot (*Poicephalus senegalus*): *Size:* $9\frac{1}{2}$ inches (24 cm). *Distribution:* Western Africa in 3 subspecies. *Clutch:* 2–3 white eggs. *Incubation:* 22–23 days. *Fledging:* 9–11 weeks. This is a very popular species due to the fact that it quickly becomes tame and affectionate. It is a good talker and mimic. The best breeding results will be obtained in an outdoor aviary with a nest box $12 \times 12 \times 20$ inches ($30 \times 30 \times 50$ cm); entrance: 5 inches ($12\frac{1}{2}$ cm).

Blue-fronted Amazon (*Amazona aestiva*): *Size:* $14\frac{1}{2}$ inches (37 cm). *Distribution:* Brazil, Bolivia, and northern Argentina. There are 2 subspecies. *Clutch:* 2–4 white eggs. *Incubation:* 27–29 days. Fledging: 2 months. Provide a hollow tree trunk, a barrel, or a nest box of thick hardwood timber, $24 \times 12 \times 12$ inches ($62 \times 30 \times 30$ cm); entrance: 6 inches (15 cm). Breeding successes are

Left: African gray; right: Senegal parrot.

Selected Popular Pet Birds

Top: blue and gold macaw; center: blue–fronted Amazon; bottom: Cuvier's toucan.

plentiful, although most pairs are often aggressive towards other large hookbills. They adapt very well to cage life. Most Amazons, but especially this species, have amusing personalities, and easily learn to repeat words and short sentences, although they don't match the talent of an African gray parrot. The blue-fronted Amazon is imported regularly. The various subspecies of the yellow-fronted Amazon (*Amazona ochrocephala*) are the only other Amazons that are regularly imported.

Finches and Related Seed-eating Birds

With a few exceptions, the exotic seed-eating birds—which are readily available—are easier to keep in cages and aviaries than canaries or budgerigars. This is not to say that such birds do not require just as much care and management as our two most popular kinds of cage or aviary birds! But given suitable accommodation and a varied diet (see page 45), these birds will reward us by remaining in top condition and breeding readily.

Most species will do well, in both indoor cages or outdoor aviaries. You must, however, take into account that the majority of these birds come from countries with milder climates than our own, and that newly imported birds require warmth. Once they are acclimated—or if they are birds born and reared here—they may be placed in an outdoor aviary up to the end of September, provided part of the roof is covered and a draft-free night shelter is available. In winter, they are best kept indoors at a temperature of not less than 50°F (10°C); for some species an even higher temperature is necessary.

Finches are sociable birds. You must not, as with soft-billed birds, attempt to keep one alone, otherwise the bird will eventually pine away. This is not to say that large numbers of birds should be kept together; with a few exceptions, pairs are aggressive toward others of their own species, especially if there is a shortage of nesting sites. In large cages or preferably in an aviary or a room aviary, it is possible to keep several pairs together, but then only one pair from each species. Moreover, there must be room enough for the birds to keep out of each other's way and there must be a choice of at least two roosting boxes for each pair, to avoid squabbling. These roosting boxes may in many cases be used as nesting sites, but naturally, you must also provide wire baskets and various nest boxes (see illustrations, page 115).

Once the birds are fully acclimated they can be placed in an outdoor aviary, but here also you must avoid overcrowding. If you want successful breeding, each pair requires a ground area of 2 to 3 square meters—depending on the size of the birds. The moment there is a risk of frost, the birds should be brought indoors—unless you can supply a well-lit and guaranteed frost-free shelter with plenty of flying room. The aviary walls near the shelter may be covered with plastic sheeting for further protection. If birds are overwintered indoors, they must also be protected from excessive cold, and extra light should be provided on dark winter nights so that they receive their daily quota of food before roosting for the night. For this, you can use Vita Lite (see page 36), which can be left on during the darker part of the day. The lights should be protected with mesh so that the birds cannot come into contact with them and injure themselves. The same goes for any heating appliances used in winter quarters, otherwise you may lose some birds—if not the whole stock—from burns.

If, in spite of providing proper accommodations, your foreign finches fail to breed, this may be because of an inadequate diet. In the wild, these birds consume a variety of unripe and ripe seeds, as well as insects and green food. A good and varied diet (see page 45) is therefore the first factor. In the summer you can hang ripe and unripe seeding grasses, plantain, corn, etc., in the aviary so that the birds can serve themselves. Seed used for soaking (see page 42) should be of the best quality and may be prepared as discussed earlier (see page 42). Alternatively, half fill a jelly jar with seed, fill with warm water, and leave overnight. The following morning pour off the excess water and spread the seed on a cloth. As soon as the first sprouts show, you can give it to the birds. When young birds are being reared, this food is essential. As we have already discussed, young birds of most species also require animal food: such items as ant pupae (which must be softened in water or milk if only dried forms are available), chopped mealworms, maggots, very young cockroaches, a good rearing food, unsalted and unseasoned fresh hard-boiled egg—all mixed together with bread or biscuit crumbs. You must also ensure that calcium is contained in the diet in the form of fine oyster shell, grit, ground eggshell, or cuttlefish bone. If your birds lay well but do not brood, or brood but not

Top: a basket and two nest boxes for finches; bottom: a home-made, small but efficient breeding cage for just one pair of finches or parakeets.

rear their young satisfactorily, then you can use society finches (Bengalese) or zebra finches as foster parents for the more expensive or difficult species (for example, Australian grass finches).

True Finches

Green Singing Finch (*Serinus mozambicus*): *Size:* 5 inches (12 cm). *Distribution:* Africa, south of the Sahara. *Clutch:* 3–4 pale-blue eggs. *Incubation:* 14 days; only the female incubates. *Fledging:* 18 days. Plenty of live food is essential as well as canary-rearing food. In the breeding season, males often become spiteful toward small waxbills, except in a spacious, well-planted garden aviary. The male has a clear and sweet song. Young females have a "necklace" of 5 to 7 small black spots across the throat. This species pairs only for the breeding season, and afterward separates. They use an open-type nest box or a free cup-shaped nest and will breed more readily in large cages or roomy indoor aviaries where a reasonably warm temperature can be maintained. Hybrids between a male finch × female border or roller canary are very possible.

Gray-singing Finch (*Serinus leucopygius*): *Size:* 4½ inches (11½ cm). *Distribution:* Northeastern and equatorial Africa. *Clutch:* 3–4 very pale-green to white eggs. Incubation: 14–16 days. *Fledging:* 18–22 days. The male is an excellent singer, especially during the breeding season. The species has a playful nature and is fine for a well-planted garden aviary with other small birds (waxbills, mannikins, etc.). They like to use an open-type nest box or a canary nest pan. Hybrids have been produced between cock finch × hen (border) canary.

Yellow-rumped Seedeater or Black-throated Canary (*Serinus atrogularis*): *Size:* 6 inches (15 cm). *Distribution:* Africa. *Clutch:* 3–4 blue eggs with red-brown markings. *Incubation:* 14–15 days. *Fledging:* 14–16 days. Excellent in a mixed-bird collection! Their singing abilities are quite good but don't match those of the gray-singing finch.

Alario Finch or Black-headed Canary (*Serinus alario*): *Size:* 5½ inches (14 cm). *Distribution:* South Africa. *Clutch:* 2–5 pale-blue eggs with red-brown markings. *Incubation:* 14–17 days; incubated by both parents. *Fledging:* 18–20 days. The active male has a soft warbling song and hybridizes easily with a hen canary. They use half-open nest boxes which should be placed close to the ground. Both sexes feed their young.

Buntings

Saffron Finch (*Sycalis flaveola*): *Size:* 6 inches (15 cm). *Distribution:* South America, from Venezuela to southern Brazil. In Jamaica, where the species was introduced in 1823, it is known as the wild canary. *Clutch:* 3–4 white eggs with light-gray markings. *Incubation:* 14 days; incubated by the female. *Fledging:* 14 days. Young birds receive their final coloring after their third year; their first molt occurs after 4–6 months. Throughout the year insects as well as greens are essential. This species

is a suitable companion for weavers, Java sparrows, and other similar bird, especially during the breeding season, when housed in a small, crowded aviary. The species will use a canary nest pan or half-open nest box, or build a free cup-shaped nest in a thick bush. They are often somewhat rambunctious toward smaller birds.

Cardinals and Grosbeaks

Red-crested Cardinal (*Paroaria coronata*): *Size:* 7½ inches (19 cm). *Distribution:* Southern Brazil and Argentina to Bolivia. *Clutch:* 3–4 white eggs with gray markings. *Incubation:* 14 days; both parents incubate. *Fledging:* 14 days. This bird has a cheerful disposition and likes to brood in half-open nest boxes close to the ground (about 63 inches [150 cm]).

Green Cardinal (*Gubernatrix cristata*): *Size:* 7½ inches (19 cm). *Distribution:* Argentina, Uruguay, and southeastern Brazil. *Clutch:* 3–4 blue-green eggs with dark markings. *Incubation:* 12–14 days; only the hen incubates. *Fledging:* 14 days. Live food is essential, especially in the breeding season. This species has hybridized a few times with the red-crested cardinal—a remarkable cross, as both birds belong to a different genus!

Cuban Finch (*Tiaris canora*): *Size:* 4 inches (10 cm). *Distribution:* Cuba, Haiti, Jamaica, and surrounding islands. *Clutch:* 3–5 blue-white eggs. *Incubation:* 11–13 days. *Fledging:* 12–17 days. It is advisable to keep only one pair in a community aviary. The Cuban finch is a free breeder and prefers to nest low in brushwood or in a thick bush. The domed nest has a tunnel-shaped entrance. Remove the young as soon as they can look after themselves (this is after approximately one month). The male is often very belligerent, even toward birds twice or three times his size!

Weavers and Whydahs

Grenadier Weaver, Orange Bishop or Red Bishop (*Euplectes orix*): *Size:* 5 inches (12 cm).

Distribution: Africa, south of the Sahara. *Clutch:* 2–4 green-blue eggs. *Incubation:* 12 days; only the female incubates. *Fledging:* 14 days. Live food is a must. The nest is oval in shape and composed of reed blades, and is slung between upright reeds or branches. In the wild as well as in captivity, the female does the feeding and rearing of the young, while the male guards the nest. Colony breeder.

Madagascar Weaver (*Foudia madagascariensis*): *Size:* 5 inches (12 cm). *Distribution:* Malagasy Republic, Reunion, Mauritius, Seychelles. *Clutch:* 3–5 pale-blue eggs. *Incubation:* 14 days; incubated by the female. The male does all the nest building. *Fledging:* 14 days. The hen feeds the chicks. Live food, soft-billed birds' rearing food, and seeding grass are essential throughout the year but especially during the breeding season. The free nest is built in thick bushes, although finch and parakeet nest boxes are frequently used. Often the birds will breed four or more times per season in the same nest box.

Red-billed Weaver (*Quela quela*): *Size:* 5 inches (12 cm). *Distribution:* Africa, south of the Sahara. *Clutch:* 3–5 blue-green eggs. *Incubation:* 14 days; the female incubates. The cock is an industrious builder, and is always willing to play the architect. The end result is a ball-shaped nest. Successful breeding is possible as long as one has at least two pairs in a large garden aviary. Live food is essential. *Fledging:* 14 days. Dr. Arthur Butler, our representative of the Victorian age of aviculture, writes: "When building, they will let no other weaver approach them, but will raise their wings almost to their heads, and use shocking language at the intruder. But when weary of this work, they rest on a branch at a short distance, and any bird may meddle with the nest with impunity, unless it so happens that the working fit comes on again, whilst some meddlesome fellow is trying to discover how it is put together, when there is sure to be a charge, a chase, and much chattering, but nothing worse." It is advisable to house this bird, as well as similar species—such as the crimson-crowned bishop

Top: Pekin robin. Bottom, left to right: the Napoleon weaver (*Euplectus afra*) from Africa, south of the Sahara, is a hardy and amiable species (for more details see the grenadier weaver); a superb or orange–rumped tanager; and a green cardinal.

(*Euplectes hordeacea*) and golden bishop, yellow-crowned weaver, or black and yellow-colored Napoleon weaver (*E. afer*) in a large garden aviary.

Pin-tailed Whydah (*Vidua macroura*): *Size:* 5 inches (12 cm). The elongated tail feathers ("widow's weeds") of a fully developed male are about 10 inches (24 cm). *Distribution:* Africa, south of the Sahara. *Clutch:* 3–4 white eggs. This species is the only "true whydah" or widow-bird that (like many cuckoos) parasitizes more than one species: the orange-cheeked waxbill (*Estrilda melpoda*), the red-eared waxbill (*E. troglodytes*), and the St. Helena waxbill (*E. astrild*) are among the approximately 19 species acting as hosts! In nuptial plumage the hardy and lively male is often spiteful toward other aviary birds, so a pair is best kept with somewhat larger pet birds. Live food is essential.

Queen or Shaft-tailed Whydah (*Vidua regia*): *Size:* 5 inches (12 cm). In full plumage, with four central elongated tail-feathers, the male is about 13

inches (32 cm). *Distribution:* South Africa. *Clutch:* 3–4 white eggs. The host species is the violet-eared waxbill (*Uraeginthus granatina*). Single males are peaceful toward other birds but will become quarrelsome when kept in pairs. Live food forms an important part of the diet.

Paradise Whydah (*Vidua or Steganura paradisea*): *Size:* 6 inches (15 cm). *Distribution:* Eastern and southern Africa, in various subspecies. *Clutch:* 3–4 white eggs. This striking bird, which in full plumage measures approximately 20 inches (50 cm), parasitizes three races of the melba finch (*Pytilia melba, P. grotei,* and *P. soudanensis*). The species is a peaceful and hardy bird. It is advisable, however, to house the bird in a large garden or indoor aviary.

Sparrows

Golden Sparrow (*Passer luteus*): *Size:* 5½ inches (14 cm). *Distribution:* Northeast Africa. *Clutch:* 3–4 light-green eggs. Incubation: 10–13 days; incubated only by the female. *Fledging:* 14 days. An excellent bird for a community aviary, especially when kept in several pairs. Males are sometimes spiteful toward each other and other birds.

Estrildid Finches

Cutthroat Finch (*Amadina fasciata*): *Size:* 5 inches (12 cm). *Distribution:* Africa, south of the Sahara. *Clutch:* 4–9 eggs. Incubation: 12–14 days; both sexes incubate. *Fledging:* 18–20 days. These finches tend to pester other breeding pairs. They visit their nests, causing a certain disquiet that may lead the other birds to abandon their nests. A breeding pair prefers a half-open nest box. Insects and sprouted seeds are essential year round. Be sure to provide this bird with a steady supply of minerals and cuttlefish bone, since the female is rather susceptible to egg binding (see page 75).

Red-headed Finch (*Amadina erythrocephala*): *Size:* 5¼ inches (13 cm). *Distribution:* Africa, from South Africa northward to Angola and Natal. *Clutch:* 3–6 eggs. *Incubation:* 12–13 days; both sexes incubate. *Fledging:* 23–25 days. It is advisable to house a single pair in a separate, roomy aviary, breeding cage, or vitrine with adequate plantings, so the bird can brood successfully and in peace. This species has hybridized with the cutthroat finch, and the hybrids are fertile. For more details see *A. fasciata.*

African Golden-breasted Waxbill (*Amandava subflava*): *Size:* 3½ inches (9 cm). *Distribution:* Africa. *Clutch:* 3–6 eggs. *Incubation:* 11–13 days. *Fledging:* 22–24 days. The species must spend the winter in warm conditions (65°F [18°C]). A cheerful and friendly bird. During the breeding season, small insects, greens (especially sprouted niger seed), and millet spray are essential.

Red Avadavat, Tiger Finch, or Strawberry Finch (*Amandava amandava*): *Size:* 4 inches (10 cm). *Distribution:* India, Pakistan, South Nepal, Southeast Asia, and Indonesia. *Clutch:* 4–6 eggs. Incubation: 11–13 days. *Fledging:* 20–21 days. The species uses half-open nest boxes but is more likely to build a free keg-shaped nest in a thick bush or in ivy. During the breeding season insects are essential. Recent federal laws ban these birds from the United States.

Star Finch (*Bathilda or Neochmia ruficauda*): *Size:* 4 inches (10 cm). *Distribution:* Northern Australia. *Clutch:* 3–5 eggs. *Incubation:* 13 days. *Fledging:* 22–25 days. This species is easy to breed, provided it is kept in a well-planted (grass, reeds, ivy, dense bushes), quiet aviary. Don't disturb the birds while they are breeding, as they are quite sensitive. During the year, but especially in the breeding season, a rich variety of insects, greens, rearing food, as well as vitamins, and minerals must be available.

Gouldian Finch (*Chloebia gouldiae*): *Size:* 5¼ inches (14 cm). *Distribution:* Northern Australia, especially the Kimberley district. *Clutch:* 5–6 eggs, sometimes more. *Incubation:* 14–16 days. *Fledging:* 21–24 days. The first molt occurs at 8–10 weeks; at 5 months, the young show adult colors. A pair needs a half-open nest box of at least $6 \times 6 \times 10$ inches ($15 \times 15 \times 25$ cm), with an entrance of 2 inches (5 cm). Nesting materials are dry or fresh grass and hay, leaf veins, sisal rope, and coconut fibers. Don't furnish material in lengths greater than approximately 4 inches (10 cm). The best breeding results occur at temperatures above 77°F (25°C). To achieve a good molt, the temperature should never drop below 72°F (22°C). Sick birds should be isolated and kept at a temperature of at least 77° (25°C); in my experience a constant 86°F (30°C) is best. During molt, birds are very sensitive to temperature changes and will even stop the molt if temperatures drop below 70°F (21°C). Humidity also is extremely important; at a temperature of 77°F (25°C), the humidity should be kept at 70%. You should have a good thermometer and hygrometer to monitor the environment.

Painted Fire-tailed Finch (*Emblema picta*): *Size:* 4 inches (10 cm). *Distribution:* Australia. *Clutch:* 4–5 eggs. *Incubation:* 16–18 days. *Fledging:* 20–25 days. This species builds nests in the plantings or in canary nest pans and boxes, provided they are placed low to the ground. It tends to use rough material (bark, leaves, etc.) which is made into the foundation. The walls of the nest are made of small twigs, grass, leaf veins, and the like. For padding on the inside, it uses all types of small, soft feathers.

Black-cheeked Waxbill (*Estrilda erythronotos*): *Size:* 4 inches (10 cm). *Distribution:* East and southern Africa. *Clutch:* 3–6 eggs. *Incubation:* 12–13 days. *Fledging:* 15–17 days. The birds build a free keg-shaped nest, but also make use of various nest boxes and baskets. The species is particularly sensitive to dampness. Success in breeding is dependent on a good source of insects for food. In the winter months, house the birds in a lightly heated facility, preferably with an infrared light.

Orange-cheeked Waxbill (*Estrilda melpoda*): *Size:* 4 inches (10 cm). *Distribution:* Africa, Sene-

Top (left to right): Gouldian finch, Java sparrow, and red-cheeked cordon bleu. Bottom: Male and female pin-tailed parrot finches.

gal and neighboring countries. *Clutch:* 3–4, sometimes up to 7 white eggs. *Incubation:* 11–12 days. *Fledging:* 14–18 days. These are nervous birds that need insects during the rearing period. These birds have an oval nest with a little tunnel-like entrance. In the aviary they often like to use closed or half-open nesting boxes in which they build a ball-shaped structure. The young assume their full plumage after the first molt, which is after approximately 7 weeks.

Common Waxbill or St. Helena Waxbill (*Estrilda astrild*): *Size:* 4½ inches (11½ cm). *Distribution:* Africa, south of the Sahara; Malagasy Republic; Mauritius, St. Helena, and New Caledonia; this species is now feral in Portugal and parts of Spain. *Clutch:* 1–4 white eggs. *Incubation:* 10–13 days; incubated by both parents. *Fledging:* 14–15 days. The cock builds a bullet-shaped nest of which the top part is a false chamber. Live food is essential, especially during the breeding season.

Red-eared Waxbill (*Estrilda troglodytes*): *Size:* 4 inches (10 cm). *Distribution:* Northern Africa, from Senegal to Ethiopia. Clutch: 3–5 eggs. *Incubation:* 11–12 days; incubated by both sexes. *Fledging:* 14 days. They require a lot of insect food and fresh bathing water daily. This bird prefers to breed in garden aviaries with thick plantings and a variety of nest boxes. Hybrids are possible with society finches, St. Helena waxbills, blue-breasted waxbills, and blue-headed waxbills. Toward the end of the summer, this species is best housed in an indoor aviary or large cage. Without animal protein, they will not breed successfully.

Pin-tailed Parrot Finch (*Erythrura prasina*): *Size:* 5½ inches (13 cm). *Distribution:* From Burma through Malaysia to Sumatra, Borneo, and Java (Indonesia). *Clutch:* 4–5 eggs. *Incubation:* 13–14 days; incubated by both sexes. *Fledging:* 22–24 days. Successful breeding is a real task, especially because the birds molt twice a year. The molt, however, goes fast, lasting about 2–3 weeks. The couple builds a sizable nest from fibers, grass, leaves, leaf veins, and the like. They rarely use nest boxes. The temperature must be maintained at around 77°F (25°C), and infrared light should be used during the entire brooding period. I have found that it is best to keep three to five pairs in a single roomy aviary to achieve successful breeding.

Red-billed Firefinch (*Lagonosticta senegala*): *Size:* 3½ inches (9 cm). *Distribution:* Western Africa. *Clutch:* 3–4 eggs. *Incubation:* 11–12 days; incubated by the female. *Fledging:* 16–18 days, but the young will still be fed by their parents for another 18–20 days. Both sexes are in the "building trade." The nest is quite roughly constructed and bullet-shaped. This species will also use nesting boxes, old weaver and finch nests, and will even build a nest under the eaves. In an indoor aviary they will also breed during the winter months, but then you should not allow them to continue breeding in

the summer!

Society Finch or Bengalese (*Lonchura striata var. domestica*): *Size:* 4½ inches (11 cm). *Distribution:* This species is *not* found in the wild. *Clutch:* 5–7 eggs. *Incubation:* 20–21 days; incubated by both sexes. *Fledging:* 20–24 days. Excellent foster parents, especially for Australian grass finches. Foster nestlings should be returned to their natural parents once they reach adulthood, otherwise, these young birds will want to stay near their foster parents and won't associate with their own kind. Such imprinting should be prevented if one intends to breed the birds later. Bengalese should be provided with a breeding cage of adequate size or a spacious aviary. When the young are no longer being fed by their parents—approximately 40 days after fledging—they can be removed and placed in a large box cage. Young birds should not be used for breeding until they are at least one year old. Nest box: 10 × 10 × 10 inches (25 × 25 × 25 cm). Supply ample nesting material: coconut fibers and grass.

African Silverbill (*Lonchura malabarica cantans*): *Size:* 4½ inches (11 cm). *Distribution:* Western and central Africa. *Clutch:* 3–4 eggs. *Incubation:* 12–15 days; incubated by both sexes. *Fledging:* 21 days. These birds are excellent foster parents and will do very well in a peaceful aviary. During the winter take them indoors and place them in an unheated area. The hen of the Indian silverbill (*L. m. malabarica*)—from India, Afghanistan, and Sri Lanka—lays up to 12 eggs and has a white rump. These species are also adorable chatterboxes, like their cousins from Africa.

White-headed Munia (*Lonchura maja*): *Size:* 5 inches (12 cm). *Distribution:* Malay Peninsula and neighboring islands. *Clutch:* 4–5 eggs. *Incubation:* 12–13 days. *Fledging:* 20–21 days. This species, as well as the tricolored munia (*L. malacca*) and the black-headed munia (*L. atricapilla*), will only breed very sporadically. The birds will not tolerate scrutiny during the breeding cycle. Supply them with perches high up in the aviary, and offer them plenty of insects, cuttlebone, weed seeds, egg food, greens, canary-rearing food, and stale bread soaked in milk or water.

Spice Bird' or Spice Finch (*Lonchura punctulata*): *Size:* 4½ inches (11 cm). *Distribution:* India, Sri Lanka, southeastern Asia, southern China, Taiwan, and Hainan, through the Greater and Lesser Sundas (except Borneo) to Sulawesi and the Philippines; introduced into Australia 1942–43. Clutch: 4–7, sometimes 10 white eggs. *Incubation:* 13–14 days; incubated by both parents. *Fledging:* 21 days. The male stands out because of his very soft song, with head held high and puffed throat feathers. Hens have a tendency to suffer from egg binding (see page 75).

Common Quail Finch (*Ortygospiza atricollis*): *Size:* 4 inches (10 cm). *Distribution:* Africa, south of the Sahara to Angola and Damaraland. *Clutch:* 4–6 eggs. *Incubation:* 11–12 days. *Fledging:* 14–16 days, but the young will still be fed by their parents for another 2–3 weeks. These small terrestrial birds often fly perpendicularly, so it is necessary to attach some soft material against the inside of the cage's roof. The aviary floor can best be covered with high grasses. It is ill-advised to keep other ground-dwellers, like the Chinese painted quail, in the same community aviary.

Java Sparrow (*Padda oryzivora*): *Size:* 5½ inches (14 cm). *Distribution:* Java and Bali. Introduced into Sri Lanka, southern Burma, Zanzibar, St. Helena, among other places. *Clutch:* 3–5 eggs. *Incubation:* 12–15 days. *Fledging:* 26–28 days. Keeping Java sparrows in captivity is illegal in various parts of the United States, as escaped birds could become a serious threat to agriculture. Well-known mutations are white, pied (calico), and black-headed; these mutations are extremely popular in Europe. Do not hang the half-open nest boxes (12 × 10 × 10 inches [30 × 25 × 25 cm]) too close together in order to avoid fighting. Beechwood blocks (entrance: 2 inches [5 cm]) are excellent! If the aviary is fairly peaceful with only a few fellow inhabitants, breeding success is guaranteed. If nothing is done to prevent it, Java sparrows will breed throughout the year, which of course could lead to egg-binding problems. Limit the breeding period from May through July and no more than four clutches per season.

Long-tailed Finch (*Poephila acuticauda*): *Size*: 7 inches (18 cm). *Distribution*: Northern and northwestern parts of Australia. *Clutch*: 5–6 eggs. *Incubation*: 13 days. *Fledging*: 20–22 days. Give the birds as many different nest boxes as possible; they must be positioned high behind natural cover and far apart. The birds will construct roosting nests as well, so be sure to provide enough building materials. Sometimes different pairs will sleep together in those nests.

Masked Finch (*Poephila personata*): *Size*: 5 inches (12 cm). *Distribution*: Northern Australia. *Clutch*: 4–6 eggs. *Incubation*: 13 days. *Fledging*: 20–22 days. An excellent, sociable, but noisy bird, which needs a large, well-planted aviary. Its nest is bulky, close to the ground, and constructed from grass, small feathers, plant fibers, and wool.

Melba Finch (*Pytilia melba*): *Size*: 5 inches (12 cm). *Distribution*: Africa, south of the Sahara. *Clutch*: 3–4 eggs. *Incubation*: 12 days. *Fledging*: 20–21 days. This species is known to be aggressive toward other small birds, especially during the breeding season. I feel it necessary to house this species indoors at room temperature in separate accommodations. Throughout the year a variety of seeds, vitamins and minerals, and, especially, various insects, are necessary.

Zebra Finch (*Taeniopygia* or *Poephila guttata*): *Size*: 4 inches (10 cm). *Distribution*: Australia, except the coastal areas of Victoria and New South Wales. A subspecies is found on the island of Timor. *Clutch*: 4–5, sometimes up to 10 white eggs. *Incubation*: 13–16 days; both partners take turns in hatching the eggs. *Fledging*: 20–22 days. Zebra finches not only demand little in the way of care but they are also easy to breed. The male has a bright and vigorous trumpeting song. They offer endless opportunities to achieve fascinating color mutations through color-breeding experimentation.

Selected Popular Pet Birds

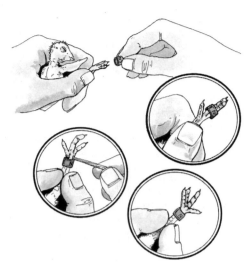

Banding a chick. Take the bird's foot between your fingers in such a manner that the back toe points toward the back and the other toes are stretched together toward the front. Rub a *little* petroleum jelly, salad oil, or saliva on the toes. Now place the band over the three front toes, slide it backwards, over the back toe, and continue a little further up the leg as well. If the back toe is still "trapped" under the band, release it with a somewhat pointed matchstick. The band is now correctly positioned around the chick's leg. After you clean the leg, put back the chick into the nest.

Zebra finches are prolific breeders in garden aviaries, but to avoid egg binding (see page 75) and weak young, the number of broods should be limited to three per season. Remove all nesting material (grass, plant fibers, feathers, moss, wool) as soon as the nest is completed, to prevent further construction. The free nest is bottle-shaped, with an entrance tunnel. Zebra finches like to use all types of nest boxes. Young females should not be used for breeding until they are at least 9 to 10 months of age. The cocks and hens should be separated during the winter, preferably housed indoors in an unheated but frost-free area. Three weeks after the young

have flown out, they can be considered to be independent and can be taken away from their parents so that the hen can start on a new brood. Hang the nest boxes near the roof of the cage or aviary to prevent the birds from making another nest on top of it!

Red-cheeked Cordon Bleu (*Uraeginthus bengalus*): *Size*: 5 inches (12 cm). *Distribution*: Africa, from Senegal to Ethiopia and south through eastern Africa to Zambia. *Clutch*: 4–5 white eggs. *Incubation*: 11–13 days; incubated by both sexes. *Fledging*: 17 days. Live food is essential, especially in the breeding season. This species prefers to breed in garden aviaries with thick plantings and a variety of nest boxes. Hybrids are possible with society finches, St. Helena waxbills, blue-breasted waxbills, and blue-headed waxbills. Toward the end of the summer, this bird is best housed in an indoor aviary or large cage.

Violet-eared Waxbill (*Uraeginthus granatina*): *Size*: 4½ inches (11 cm). *Distribution*: Africa, from Angola to Zambia. *Clutch*: 3–6 white eggs. *Incubation*: 13–15 days; incubated by both parents. *Fledging*: 17–18 days. Live food and finchrearing food are essential throughout the year, but especially during the breeding season. After the acclimation period the birds may be placed in garden aviaries, provided the outside temperature is no less than 68°F (20°C). Although generally friendly, these birds are often hostile and aggressive toward members of the same genus. If various finches are kept in the same facility, a well-planted aviary is the answer. I recommended breeding in indoor aviaries, as during the first few days the young birds don't have much down; temperatures below 77°F (25°C) are often fatal!

Diamond Sparrow (*Zonaeginthus or Emblema guttata*): *Size*: 5 inches (12 cm). *Distribution*: Eastern Australia. *Clutch*: 5–6 eggs. *Incubation*: 12–14 days; incubated by both parents. *Fledging*: 25–30 days. Temperatures below 60°F (15°C) are not well tolerated; birds housed in outdoor quarters must be put inside in early fall as soon as temperatures start to drop. Pairs need a good selection of nesting

Selected Popular Pet Birds

materials: coconut fibers, leaf veins, wool, moss, and soft dry grass (up to 20 inches [50 cm] long!), but watch out for long pieces of thread and string, since the parents and the young can get tangled in it. A free-standing bullet-shaped nest is usually constructed in a thick bush; the nest often has a long entrance tunnel. The birds also use various nest boxes. Independent young must be housed in a separate flight, as the male parent often aggressively chases them around.

Bicheno's Finch or Owl Finch (*Stizoptera bichenovii*): *Size*: 3 inches (8 cm). *Distribution*: Australia. *Clutch*: 4–5 white eggs. *Incubation*: 14 days; incubated by both parents. *Fledging*: 22 days. This extremely friendly and peaceful aviary bird needs some live food throughout the year, but especially during the breeding season. Breeding should be successful, provided you have a true pair and the aviary is not crowded. This species builds its own little nest from grass and feathers in thick shrubbery, or uses a nesting box. The birds are often found on the ground, and it is advisable to have a leaf-mold compost heap in one of the corners of the aviary. This heap should give the birds the opportunity to look for insects, satisfying their urge for scratching.

Quail

Together with pheasants, partridges, the peafowl, and our own domestic fowl, quail belong to a large bird family known as the *Phasianidae*, which has approximately 60 genera and some 180 species in great variety, from the Chinese painted quail to the imposing peacock.

Foreign quail, which are imported in several species, are known as ground birds. They can be kept indoors or outdoors in aviaries which contain a collection of tree birds. They are fairly easy to keep in such conditions and breed readily, although the Chinese painted quail will also breed in a show case or indoor cage. In the winter, all species must

be kept indoors—not that they cannot stand dry cold, but they are unable to tolerate the damp and misty periods of our winters. In the aviary, they will eat the seed dropped on the ground by the other birds. If you give them a daily helping of a good seed mix (for instance, adequate for finches—see page 44), universal food, and a few small mealworms, the birds should do well. If you keep quail in an indoor show case, you should provide one or two grass sods which can be frequently changed, so that the birds have something to peck at. In the grassy outdoor aviary, quail should be provided with a tray of fine, clean, and dry sand, so that they can take a sand bath whenever they wish.

If you keep quail in a separate accommodation where they cannot benefit from seed dropped by other birds, you should supply a basic food consisting of a mixture of millet, canary-grass seed, and a few weed seeds, complemented by green food, seeding grasses, and daily, a few small mealworms or maggots.

One of the nicest and most frequently imported species is the Chinese painted quail (*Excalfactoria chinensis*), which comes from India and southern China. It stands no taller than $4^1/_2$ inches (11 cm), and the sexes are easy to distinguish. Like most quail, this species has a habit of suddenly flying vertically into the air when alarmed and, if they should fly into the roof of the cage, there is a danger of severe injury. To prevent injury, it is advisable to install a layer of sacking just under the roof mesh of the cage, and a couple of inches below this, a fine meshed netting—something of the sort that petticoats are made from. In the wild, the Chinese painted quail lives in pairs and you cannot keep two pairs in the same accommodation without the risk of the cocks fighting to the death! In order to prevent the cock from putting the female off breeding with his fiery, territorial behavior, many breeders run a cock with two or three hens and remove him as soon as the hens start to lay. The eggs are laid in a hollow in a concealed corner, behind low clumps of plants. The clutch consists of an average of 8 to 12 eggs, but

16 or more are not unusual. The incubation time is about 17 days. The hatchlings are so small that they can easily slip through the doubled aviary wire; therefore it is wise to place panels of glass, board, or cardboard around the bottom edge of the aviary. As described earlier, the rearing food consists of a mixture of egg and rusk, soaked bread, and is made up with a little commercial rearing food, ant pupae, and poppy seed. After two or three days, a helping of finely chopped green food can also be offered.

The young are wholly independent at about 6 weeks and the hen will begin her second clutch. The original brood can then be removed to a brood machine (it is possible to buy one which is barely larger than a radio) or alternatively, placed in an old aquarium tank and kept warm with a heat lamp. The hen can then start her second clutch in peace.

If you are rearing the chicks yourself, you must ensure that drinking water is available in a very shallow container—remembering that a chick is little bigger than a bumblebee and could easily drown in a small amount of water.

If you keep quail with other birds, the drinking vessel must be covered to prevent it from becoming soiled with droppings. Feeding and drinking containers should not be placed near the walls of the aviary, as quail tend to run up and down the edges and would run over and over again through their food and water.

Doves

With the exception of the polar regions, doves are to be found all over the world. Of the 300 or so species, there are those which are little larger than a sparrow, and others which reach the size of a ptarmigan. More than half the species live in Australia and the Indo-Malaysian archipelago—but there is also a good selection of species in Europe, and North and South America.

All doves are monogamous and proverbially

Doves prefer covered dishes!

"loving" to their mates. Their nests are flimsy affairs, consisting of not more than a few twigs laid loosely in the bough of a tree, and the clutch is very small, mostly just two eggs. These are usually a silvery white, but occasionally brown or lightly colored. In the majority of species, both cock and hen build the nest and share in the incubation of the eggs; the hen sitting during the night, the cock during the day. The incubation period varies from 14 to 19 days and the young are born with closed eyes. They stay in the nest another 12 to 18 days and are fed with a substance known as "pigeon milk"— partially digested food from the parents' crops, as well as cheesy, curdlike pieces of the crop's lining (during the incubation period the lining of the pigeon's crop thickens). The chick sticks its beak into that of the feeding parent, who regurgitates the food.

All doves have an unusual method of drinking.

Selected Popular Pet Birds

While nearly every other bird takes a beakful of water and raises the head to allow it to run into the throat, doves take water in a long draft similar in manner to a horse. They feed mainly on seeds, berries, and other fruits, but also insects; they may travel several miles from the nest in search of food for their young. They possess a fairly muscular body, thickly covered with feathers which are, however, quite loosely implanted. This is why feathers easily fall out of a dead bird. In addition to the domestic pigeon, which developed from the rock dove (not the wood pigeon, as it is commonly believed), there are a number of exotic doves frequently kept in cages and aviaries. Especially suitable is the Barbary or domestic ringdove (*Streptopelia risoria*). It has a tame nature, is easy to care for, and is a ready breeder. It is hardened to our climate and can be kept in an outdoor aviary year round. It is perfectly safe to keep together with even the smallest of other birds. It is intolerant only of its own species; the males can be particularly aggressive to each other. You can keep a pair in the house; if you do, invest in a cage approximately 5 feet (1.5 m) long, 23½ inches (60 cm) deep, and 35½ inches (90 cm) high, and allow the birds to exercise daily in the room. For nesting, you can supply a tray, approximately 8 × 4 inches (20 × 10 cm) and a few inches high. Nest materials can be given in the form of twigs and straw. An excellent seed mixture of fine grains and seeds, supplemented with green food, must be given fresh each day (see seed mixture below).

The majority of imported dove species are relatively easy to care for and to breed. One of the most popular is the Australian diamond dove (*Geopelia cuneata*), which does well in an aviary or in a cage, and breeds readily in either. In the aviary, place a gauze "nest," filled with a few twigs and some grass; in the breeding cage—which should be about 40 inches (1 m) long and 32 inches (81 cm) high—a box can be used as described for the Barbary dove. In the summer, diamond doves really feel at home in the aviary but as soon as the colder weather

Ring neck doves, incubating.

begins, they must be brought indoors and kept at a temperature of not less than 48°F (8°C). At this time it is best to separate the cocks from the hens so that the birds do not become exhausted from continuous breeding activity. Their food consists of a mixture of canary-grass seed (25%), white millet (25%), red millet (20%), niger-thistle seed (10%), sesame seed (10%), wheat (5%), and poppy (5%). As soon as young arrive both parents and offspring should also be offered universal food, rearing food, small mealworms, and ant pupae (preferably fresh). The brood usually consists of two young, normally a cock and a hen. A good breeding pair should rear three clutches each season. The incubation time is 13 days and the young leave the nest about 14 days later, when they already resemble the adults—apart from being a little smaller. After they have left the nest, the parents continue feeding them for a short time. As soon as they are eating independently they should be removed, or they may be attacked by the parents and severely wounded, if not killed. The sexes are very similar but the cock's wings are blue-gray while those of the hen are more brown-gray. Moreover, the red eye ring of the cock is narrower than that of the hen, and it is the cock bird which, from time to time, spreads his long, pointed tail.

Soft-billed Birds (Insect- and Fruit-eaters)

Those who are interested in soft-billed birds should be aware of the facts that the care of these colorful birds takes more time than, for example, seedeaters or most parrots and parakeets. The planning of their food and the daily cleaning of their various housing facilities are two things that require considerably more time than with other bird types. Cleanliness of the bird houses (aviary, bird room, cage) is and will remain extremely important if the untimely death of our little feathered friends is to be avoided. If housing and care are up to par, you will find that soft-billed birds are by no means "weak" birds, but that they can be kept for many years in top condition.

Because of their generally beautiful colors, their extremely interesting behavior, and their often wonderfully lovely song, the few birds that are dealt with in this book are a proud possession for any serious aviculturist.

It is a commonly known fact that insect-eating birds regularly eat various indigestible materials and later vomit these up in the form of a little ball. I suggest, therefore, that you mix in with the birds' food just a few small feathers that have first been cut up with a pair of scissors. If you do this twice a week, you can help the formation of the little regurgitated balls, which have something to do with the stimulation of stomach juices.

There are several very good bird feeds on the market that are suitable for all insect-eating birds, such as the Pekin robin, the shama, the white eyes, etc. The big advantage of this type of food is that dried insects have already been mixed in.

Apart from such prepared foods, it is absolutely essential to provide the birds with live food, and several possibilities have been mentioned earlier (see page 48). Keep in mind that variety can only be good for the health of your bird collection. For a change, you can offer them ground beef heart, both in cooked and raw form (though in small quantities), and you can mix in some rusk crumbs, bran, shrimp meal, beetle meal, or silkworm meal (all coarsely ground). Offer these in small quantities, of course, and refresh them twice per day. A little carrot juice or shredded apple can be added to improve the consistency; water can also be used, but carrot juice is preferable. Keep in mind, however, whether you mix these concoctions yourself or buy them ready-made from a bird-specialty store, that the consistency must not be wet. In warm weather you will need to serve fresh food more frequently.

Fruit-eaters are a little easier to feed. All kinds of soft and juicy fruits, such as apples, pears, plums, oranges, raisins, currants, bananas, figs, dates, grapes, gooseberries, black berries from the black elder or white elder, etc., are acceptable. If you look around, it will soon become apparent which foods your local birds enjoy, and it will be safe to offer these berries to your tropical birds, too. Dried berries can also be offered, but these should be soaked in water for 24 hours before they are served.

Apart from fruit, there are a great many vegetables that can be given to fruit-eating birds. The best is chickweed, followed in preference by lettuce, endive, and sprouting seedlings of "aviary" seeds. There are also quite a number of species of insect- and fruit-eating birds which enjoy a variety of seed.

Leafbirds

Fairly closely related to the bulbuls (see page 127) are the leafbirds (*Irenidae*), of which the genus Chloropsis is very important to aviculturists.

Golden-fronted Leafbird or Fruitsucker

(*Chloropsis aurifrons*): *Size*: 8 inches (20 cm). *Distribution*: Himalayan region in India and Indochina; Sri Lanka and Sumatra. *Clutch*: 2–3 reddish white eggs with red-colored markings in the form of spots, circles, and little stripes. *Incubation*: 14–16 days. *Fledging*: 17–18 days. Their free nest is cup-shaped, and made of moss, hair, stalks, leaves, long grass, hay, spider webs, coconut and hemp fibers. Usually placed in the fork of a branch. The nest is lined with little roots and moss. This enchanting species sings beautifully. They are kept as decorative birds in cages in their native lands; they become very tame, and their inquisitive nature is a source of great amusement. The species spends most of its time in the branches of trees and bushes, rarely comes on the ground, and flies very little. The molt takes place in the fall, so the birds find fluctuating temperatures difficult to tolerate. Needless to say, they should be brought indoors into a lightly heated area (about 64°F [18°C]) during the winter months.

Members of this genus have beaks that are slightly curved, strongly built, and quite long. The wings are pointed. The tail is short in comparison with the body and wings. Their feet are often greenish in color. The richness of the colors in their plumage is sometimes quite overwhelming. They have the same nutritional requirements as the bulbuls (see page 127). Sometimes they tend to make a mess at the feeding dishes, since many have the habit of carefully inspecting the contents, piece by piece. They are somewhat quick-tempered, so that some mess is usually inevitable. They enjoy bathing, and drink a lot. Some of these birds are tolerant toward small birds but not toward fellow species; this can cause some pretty serious fighting to take place. They are very suitable as both cage and aviary birds. Since the birds are very active, a cage should measure at least 31½ × 20 × 24 inches (80 × 50 × 60 cm). Remember: Always introduce a pair to their quarters together.

Orange-bellied Leafbird (*Chloropsis hardwickei*): *Size*: 8 inches (20 cm). *Distribution*: Himalayan region, Assam, Malaysia, and Burma.

Clutch: 2–3 reddish-white eggs with red spots and little stripes. *Incubation*: 14 days. *Fledging*: 17–18 days. The female hatches the eggs by herself, but both parents feed the young. In captivity, breeding is successful only on a sporadic basis. The birds were first imported into London in 1876. They sing quite well, something like a thrush, but less clear and full in tone; sometimes their song even brings a canary to mind.

A somewhat smaller bird is the lesser green leafbird (*C. cyanopogon*) from Malaysia. This bird is seldom offered for sale. Another much-kept bird, however, is the fairy blue bird (*Irena puella*) from India, Malaysia, and Indochina, which I would like to discuss. This is a really gorgeous bird. The upper part of this bird's head is blue, as are the neck, back, shoulders, and upper tail coverts. The rest of the body is a shiny black. The eyes are red, the feet are gray, and the beak is black. *Size*: 10 inches (25 cm). The hen is readily distinguishable from the male, as she is greenish-blue in color. The birds like to be housed in fairly roomy quarters, where the keeper must regularly mist the area with a plant mister; dryness plays havoc with their plumage. They enjoy a large variety of insects, a good brand universal and chick-rearing or soft foods, pieces of sweet apple, and mealworms.

Bulbuls

Bulbuls (*Pycnonotidae*) are often beautiful, colorful, and decorative birds; some species even have a rather pert crest. In both shape and behavior they are somewhat like the thrushes. These birds, which spend virtually all of their time in the trees, live mostly on fruits, especially berries, and now and then some insects. Their cup-shaped nests are suspended in trees and bushes. Ornithologists have divided the bulbuls, which come from Asia and Africa, into some 119 species. In captivity you can offer them universal food (use only trusted brands) and a good soft food; in addition to this, do not forget to include some small mealworms.

Selected Popular Pet Birds

Red-bellied Bulbul (*Pycnonotus fuscus*): *Size*: 8 inches (20 cm). *Distribution*: India and Sri Lanka. Found up to 6,500 feet (2,000 m) in the mountains. They prefer wooded country, particularly underbrush, so they are primarily birds of the forest's edge. *Clutch*: 3–4 reddish-white eggs with bright red-brown dots and markings, and a few purple-brown marks at the blunt end. *Incubation*: 12–13 days. *Fledging*: 13–14 days. The free nest is cup-shaped and built in thick bushes. Made of grass, spider webs, dry leaves, roots, hair, etc.; seldom moss. Often lined with moss roots and dry grass. The female hatches the eggs by herself, and the cock does not feed the hen while she is on the eggs, either. Later he does feed the young birds. Breeding results have been achieved in captivity. These birds prefer to use a canary nest, which they fill with a little hay, grass, and coconut fibers. The young birds must have an ample supply of ant pupae, mealworms, egg rusks, soaked raisins, dates, bananas, and apple.

Their song is quite pleasant—they are one of the few bulbuls that sing well. It covers some four notes that can be held with considerable force for minutes at a time, to be suddenly changed into little staccato but pure tones, only to end again on another longheld note, which is not necessarily the same as the first one.

The birds like freedom of movement and therefore need a lot of space—just like all bulbuls. You are well advised not to house bulbul species together with other birds, since there is a good possibility this will lead to more or less serious conflicts. In the breeding season they will even steal the young out of another bird's nest.

Red-vented Bulbul (*Pycnonotus cafer*): *Size*: 8 inches (20 cm). *Distribution*: From India to Indochina and Java; found up to 5,600 feet (1,700 m) in the mountains. *Clutch*: 3–4 white eggs with a vague red background and rich reddish-brown with purple markings at the blunt end. *Incubation*: 12–14 days. *Fledging*: 12–14 days. The free nest is cup-shaped; very deep and sturdy in its construction. The bird was first brought to Europe (London) in 1864. They are very sweet and tolerant toward fellow species and small birds, provided they are kept singly (not as a pair). During the winter months they need to be housed indoors in a lightly heated area. These birds also sing in a melodic and forceful fashion, although their song offers little variety. According to some fanciers, it soon becomes rather wearisome to the ear. All we can add to this is that there is no accounting for taste!

Red-eared Bulbul (*Pycnonotus jocosus*): *Size*: 8 inches (20 cm). *Distribution*: India to Indochina, southern China to Malaysia. Usually found in wooded areas but also in and around large cities. *Clutch*: 2–3, sometimes 4 white eggs with a red background and a great many brown and brown-red markings. *Incubation*: 12–13 days. *Fledging*: 15–17 days. The free nest is cup-shaped and beautifully structured. For building materials they use grass, moss, dry leaves, hay, coconut fibers, spider webs, and hair. They build their nest very close to the ground, especially in thick shrubbery, but seldom in trees. The female hatches the eggs by herself. The cock does not feed the hen while she is hatching the eggs, but he will later feed the young. The cock sings in a remarkable manner, but his song is quite difficult to describe. Personally, I feel it is more remarkable than beautiful. This species has been a much-loved cage and aviary bird for some time. Like all bulbuls, it is initially somewhat timid and withdrawn, but later this will disappear and it will even take food out of the keeper's hand. After fledging, the parents will continue to feed their young for about another 16–17 additional days.

White-eared Bulbul (*Pycnonotus leucotis*): *Size*: 7 inches (18 cm). *Distribution*: Iran to West Pakistan and Persia. Mostly in wooded areas and in the immediate vicinity of water. During the winter they are drawn to areas inhabited by people; they often live in large groups. *Clutch*: 2–4 whitish eggs with little red blotches, dots, and stripes. *Incubation*: 12–13 days. *Fledging*: 14–17 days. The free nest is cup-shaped and beautiful in structure. The cock does not sit on the eggs but will later feed the young. These bulbuls are lively, inquisitive birds, tame quite quickly, and are pleasant to other birds outside of the breeding period. During the breeding season, however, they are often very unpleasant and destructive, and will even interfere with nests belonging to other birds. It is an interesting fact that on a few occasions some aviary keepers have successfully managed to cross the white-eared bulbul with the red-eared bulbul. White-eared bulbuls cannot tolerate the cold very well; therefore, house them indoors in a lightly heated area during the winter months.

Pekin Robins

Both the beginner as well as the experienced aviculturist could do well by choosing to keep members of this interesting genus, because most of them will eat all kinds of tropical seed mixtures as well as insects and direct substitutes. The species that fall under the genus *Leiothrix* have about the same characteristics as babblers (*Muscicapidae, Timaliinae*; flycatchers and laughing thrushes repectively). The upper tail coverts stand out, covering about one-third of the actual tail; the covert feathers are quite broad. The tail is slightly forked or barely rounded. The bill is shorter than the skull. The feet are sturdy and have fairly large toes and nails.

Pekin Robin or Japanese Nightingale (*Leiothrix lutea*): *Size*: 6 inches (15 cm). *Distribution*: Indochina, in groups or pairs. *Clutch*: 3–4 light green-white eggs with red-brown and purple spots found primarily toward the blunt end of the egg. *Incubation*: 13 days. *Fledging*: 11–12 days. Their free nests are cup-shaped and are often located in thick bushes and made out of moss, roots, dried leaves, and stems. In captivity, they will use canary baskets, which must be placed in half-open nest boxes. They will also build their own nests; these of course are also cup-shaped and made of straw, bark, moss, and thin roots and twigs. The nest boxes should be hung in secluded locations. Do not be too sure that a couple will breed, in spite of what various books say. It seems that many people believe that the breeding cycle will take place without a hitch. Nothing is further from the truth, even though success is often possible today thanks to the many commercial foods available. Regardless, the clutches of the Pekin robin often fail. Once the birds have started nesting, you must proceed with the utmost care. Absolute rest is one of the first requirements. I recommend keeping only a few seedeaters of the same size and just a couple of weavers as coinhabitants of a large aviary. Smaller birds are constantly terrorized, while their nests are pulled apart and eggs and young destroyed. A good, thick green growth in the aviary is essential. During the breeding period we should offer them ant pupae, white worms, stale bread soaked in milk, but definitely no mealworms! It has come to light that Pekin robins that are given mealworms during the nesting and breeding season may throw their eggs or young out of the nest and start all over again.

After about 11 to 12 days, as stated, the young leave the nest but will continue to be fed by their parents for some time yet. At the time the young birds leave the nest their heads seem large and formless, and their plumage still has a great deal of down. The young birds appear larger than their parents at this point. As strange as it may sound, this is indeed the case! The young are bigger than their parents, sometimes even one-third larger. The explanation for this is that the young were very well fed while in the nest; now that they have come out and are in flight training and generally very active, a reserve of extra fat comes in very handy. This extra fat will gradually disappear, but they will be totally independent before the reserve is depleted. Young Pekin robins have a pink-red bill and their plumage reveals a lot of gray and black. The young birds often come out of the nest before they are completely feathered. It takes 70 to 80 days before they achieve their true coloring.

The Pekin robin was introduced into Europe by

the almost legendary Karl Hagenbeck in 1873. This bird deserves special attention because it makes such an excellent cage and/or aviary bird. These birds are strong, full of life, and sing beautifully. Karl Neunzig says, "The strength, freshness, attractiveness, and cheerfulness which the Pekin robin displays in his movements can also be found in his singing . . . The tones are full, dark, and heavy, without any sharp or shrill notes." These remarks, made almost 70 years ago, are still very true!

When excited, the male Pekin robin gives voice to a sharp "terrr" which may continue for a considerable period. The female is not as musically inclined and makes do with a much softer sounding "tia, tia, tia, tia, tirrr" in answer to the call of the male. We can thrill to the song of the male the year round, and it is not likely to bore us very quickly, but in a cage indoors the song may at times sound too loud and be a little irritating. I have been told nervous people in particular may be bothered by it; personally, I find this very hard to believe!

When Pekin robins are kept in a cage, it must measure at least $30 \times 18 \times 25\frac{1}{2}$ inches ($75 \times 45 \times 65$ cm). Experience has taught me that the birds do well in such a cage and their exuberant song and beautiful plumage will make even the most confirmed bird-hater enthusiastic! It is a pity, however, that more than one pair cannot be kept in a cage or aviary, as keeping more than one pair together leads to fighting. Cock and hen are very lovable together, softly picking in each other's feathers, sleeping close together, often having their wings over each other's shoulders, etc.

These birds will become tame very quickly and will often take a mealworm or a few ant pupae out of the keeper's hand. (There is no objection to giving them mealworms outside of the breeding period; cage birds which do not breed can also have them.) They are not terribly fussy with regard to their food, and even a beginning bird fancier should not be faced with too many problems. These birds require millet, canary-grass seed, maw seed, hemp, chopped boiled egg, ant pupae, berries, banana slices, chopped apple or pear, and once in a while some soaked raisins. A mixture of universal food and pet-bird-rearing food should also be on the menu, as well as soaked stale bread and grit. For greens you should serve well rinsed and drained lettuce, spinach, and chickweed.

The birds should have daily access to bathing water which has been warmed to room temperature. They will make enthusiastic use of it. The birds may remain in the outside aviary during the winter, as long as it is equipped with a night shelter that is wind- and rain-free, well-closed, can be heated, and has good sleeping nests. The molt takes place from August to September.

Silver-eared Mesia (*Leiothrix argentauris*): *Size*: 7 inches (18 cm). *Distribution*: Eastern Nepal through Indochina to Sumatra. The bird is an inhabitant of mountain forests that are densely wooded and have a lot of undergrowth. During the winter months, however, it descends to lower terrain and joins fellow species as well as other birds. *Clutch*: 3–4 light green-blue eggs with red-brown and brown spots and stains; the markings are more intensive at the blunt end of the egg. The eggs are practically impossible to distinguish from those of the Pekin robin. *Incubation*: 14 days. *Fledging*: 13–14 days. The free nest is cup-shaped and built between a few twigs, preferably in very thick small bushes or shrubs. They use dry bamboo leaves, roots (mainly for the inner lining), moss and the like. As an interesting note, they prefer to use strikingly colored roots in their nests. In the aviary they will also use canary "string nests." Nesting materials include coconut fibers, roots, and possibly pieces of bamboo leaves. Both the cock and the hen will sit on the eggs in turn, though the female does the major portion of the incubation. (They also build the nest together.)

It is a pleasant surprise that these birds have been offered on the market quite frequently during the last few years. They are fairly good breeders and generally will not bother other bird species kept together in a large community aviary. They will

Selected Popular Pet Birds

generally tolerate Pekin robins very well, and this tolerance is mutual. However, there are exceptions to the rule!

The cock has a full, deep-sounding call, and I think that their song is a little loud for keeping them indoors. Their care parallels that of the Pekin robin.

White Eyes

The large, mainly arboreal family of white eyes (*Zosteropidae*) has a wide distribution throughout Africa, Southeast Asia, and Australasia. They average 4 inches (10 cm) in length and have a green or yellow plumage with conspicuous white eye rings. These nectivore species cannot be sexed by visual means. They get along excellently when kept in groups and are friendly toward waxbills and other small species in a mixed-bird collection. It is interesting to know that according to F. Woolham escaped birds are now at pest proportions in various parts of the world, for example in parts of California and in fruit-growing districts in Australia.

Indian White Eye (*Zosterops palpebrosus*): *Size*: 4 inches (10 cm). *Distribution*: India, Sri Lanka, Indochina, and the Greater Sunda Islands. They live in the woods but can also be found at altitudes up to 5,600 feet (1,700 m). In April they leave for their breeding grounds. *Clutch*: 2–4, usually 3 green-blue eggs. *Incubation*: 10–11 days. *Fledging*: 10–13 days. Their free nest is cup-shaped and quite shallow. Located in trees and thick bushes, it is built of moss, hair, spiderwebs, plant fibers and the like. Both birds sit on the eggs. If their care is up to par, they will breed in captivity quite regularly.

These birds were imported into Germany in 1874 by the brothers Hagenbeck and are currently fairly regularly available on the market.

The pleasant, active white eyes, a family with some 85 different species, show to full advantage in a glass show case (27½ × 20 × 24 inches [70 × 50 ×60 cm]) or room aviary. They are tolerant toward other species and become very tame with their keeper,

particularly when you get into the habit of always taking care of the birds yourself. It may well happen that within a month they are eating out of your hand! And their song is not unpleasant, either.

It is well advised to always keep these birds in pairs. When kept alone they slowly pine away. I recommend a menu that offers variety. It is a good idea, however, to place their food on a small table of some sort (about 16 to 24 inches [40–60 cm] from the ground), because white eyes are rarely on the ground, instead they are found tumbling about the foliage looking for insects, larvae, berries, fruit, leafbuds, and yes, even nectar which they draw out by piercing a hole in the flower with their pointed beak.

Breeding white eyes still poses quite a few problems. The best chances for successful breeding results are in facilities where absolute peace reigns. It is preferable, too, to keep white eyes in aviaries without other birds.

As soon as a brood has become independent, they should be separated from their parents because the father may sometimes chase them in an aggressive way. It is interesting to note that the old nest is never used a second time but is sometimes partially demolished so that the birds may use some of the building materials for the new nest.

If there is sufficient protection from the elements, white eyes can spend the winter outdoors. But if it is at all possible, I would consider it preferable to allow these birds to spend the cold winter months indoors in a lightly heated area.

The striking narrow circle of white feathers around the eyes has given these birds their name. The males of most of the species have a fairly pleasant song. This, incidentally, is a good way to distinguish between the sexes, which are identical in appearance. In order to motivate these birds to breed in captivity, a wealth of small insects is necessary; this food is also necessary during the period when there are young in the nest. They also like soaked or cooked rice in addition to universal food and a mixture of small ant pupae, cupcake, and grated apples and carrots. When berries are in season, you can offer them bilberries now and then. Bananas and dried fruits can be given daily. A mashed-fruit concoction consisting of cherries, apples, pears, apricots, oranges, and dates sweetened with fruit sugar is also very much enjoyed by the birds.

The bird fancier should be on the lookout for sudden temperature fluctuations, which the birds find difficult to tolerate. Bathing is an absolute must for these species. As mentioned, you should bring white eyes indoors for the winter. Heating is not absolutely necessary, since they can take the cold quite well, but temperatures under the freezing point—especially when they continue for some time—are a different matter.

White eyes are found all over the tropical areas of Africa, southern Asia, and Australia. They have pointed, sometimes quite long beaks; rounded, fairly large wings; and a short tail which is sometimes slightly forked. They are found at altitudes up to 12,500 feet (3,800 m).

Mynah Birds and Other Starlings

Perhaps the best known of all the soft-billed birds in captivity are the mynahs (*Gracula*), which belong to the family of starlings (*Sturnidae*); so are many other tropical starling species (*Lamprotornis*, for example). They are all medium-sized passerines with slightly down-curved or straight beaks, strong feet, and iridescent plumage; some species are brightly marked. They are all strong fliers—think of our common starling (*Sturnus vulgaris*)—adapt easily, and are fairly omnivorous in their daily diet, especially the species living near man. The majority of the species nest in holes or cavities and lay white or light-blue eggs. They can be very aggressive and often become potential killers of smaller and weaker companions, especially during the breeding season.

Hill Mynah Bird (*Gracula religiosa*): *Size*: 12 to 18 inches (30–45 cm). *Distribution*: India,

Top: hill mynah bird (left) and superb spreo starling (right); Bottom: golden-fronted leafbird (left) and red-vented bulbul (right).

Burma, Ceylon, southeastern Asia, Malay Peninsula, Indonesia, and the Philippines. *Clutch*: 2–3 green-blue eggs with brown spots. *Incubation*: 14–15 days; both sexes incubate. *Fledging*: 4 weeks; the young are independent in approximately 2 months. Supply a cockatiel or starling nest box all year round, and in the breeding season supply dry leaves, hay, straw, twigs, coconut and hemp fibers as building material. The mynah is undoubtedly the best talker, and an excellent pet for fanciers of all ages! Use a large cage (18 to 20 cubic feet [.51–.57 m³] of stainless steel or galvanized metal, with a false wire bottom. Supply fruit and insects, as well as commercial mynah pellets. Mynahs love to bathe, especially in the morning. A well-balanced diet with vitamins and minerals, as well as much sunlight, are of the utmost importance, as this playful but messy species has in the past experienced convulsions more or less similar to human epileptic seizures.

Splended Glossy Starling (*Lamprotornis splendidus*): *Size*: 10 inches (25 cm). *Distribution*: Western Africa. *Clutch*: 2–3 green-blue eggs with red or dark-blue markings. *Incubation*: 14–15 days. *Fledging*: 27–29 days. All the birds in this genus come from Africa. In captivity their timid nature is soon lost, but nevertheless they will remain very active birds. It is advisable to supplement their menu with universal food, lean ground beef, rice, and fruit. The birds rarely use a nesting box; they usually prefer to use an old nest. Sometimes the hen, together with the cock, will build a roughly constructed nest with an entrance opening toward the bottom of the nest. In the wild these birds form little troops and follow the cattle herds and sheep flocks of the natives, and for understandable reasons! The cock sings during the early morning and evening hours; he is seldom heard during the rest of the day. Try hanging one or two old thrush nests in the aviary; most birds will make grateful use of them.

Superb Spreo Starling (*Lamprotornis* or *Spreo superbus*): *Size*: 8 inches (20 cm). *Distribution*: Northwest and northeastern Africa. *Clutch*: 3–4 blue-green eggs which are coverd with bright reddish-brown or blue spots. *Incubation*: 14–15 days. *Fledging*: approximately 25 days. The birds prefer to use roomy parakeet nest boxes or old thrush nests and the like. Since these birds will start breeding quite readily—provided they are kept in an aviary by themselves—the young of the first brood should be removed from their parents when it appears that a second round is being started.

Thrushes

Belonging to the subfamily *Turnidae*, which comprises some 300 species, the following two species stand out for their beautiful slender bodies, their long tails, and their exquisite vocal abilities. They are hardy, willing to breed, and largely insectivorous.

Shama (*Copsychus malabaricus*): *Size*: 9 to 11 inches (23–28 cm). *Distribution*: India and Indochina, with about 20 subspecies in Sri Lanka, Burma, Thailand, China, and Malaysia. *Clutch*: 4–5 (seldom 3 or 6) eggs that vary in color: blue, green, gray-blue, etc. There are a great many markings and dots in brown. *Incubation*: 11–12 days. *Fledging*: 12–13 days. The nest is cup-shaped. In the wild they use holes and cracks, especially in bamboo. In the aviary they prefer little nesting boxes that are care-

fully lined with moss, hair, hemp, fibers, small twigs, and little pieces of fabric. An occasional male may sit on the eggs, but this is quite rare. In other words, the hen generally does the hatching by herself. It is also rare for the male to feed his hen on the nest. The hen feeds the young herself, both when they fly out and while they are still on the nest. Only after about 30 days will the young birds be able to eat independently. It is best to separate them from their parents at that time.

The older birds need a roomy aviary, particularly if you plan to breed them. Before and during mating the birds are very restless and chase each other a great deal. It is therefore more sensible to house the couple by itself, or not much will come of the broods of the other birds. Once the birds are acclimated, they can spend the winter in a draft-free aviary, provided there is a night shelter that offers them protection from the elements.

They are pleasant birds to keep. In addition to being a good imitator of various thrush and nightingale songs, and even of less pleasant noises—such as a creaking, poorly-oiled wheelbarrow I once had!—the male is a sweet, pleasant-to-keep, attractive bird. He will sing and imitate with exuberance the whole year around, except during the molt. My male bird will take a mealworm out of my hand every morning. If you wish to maintain them in good condition, give them egg, caterpillars (without hair!), raw ground beef, universal food, thrush food, earthworms, grasshoppers, beetles, and white worms. It speaks for itself that the chick-rearing food for the young birds also consists mainly of insects and direct substitutes.

I have said that these birds will breed in large aviaries; however, there are a few strings attached. For one thing, they can be a nuisance toward smaller birds. Another problem is that the parent birds should have a continual supply of insects. You can let them be free to fly in the garden, but you are then unconditionally tied to keeping them in bird housing not used for any other birds. To avoid these problems you can house a breeding pair in a separate large parakeet-breeding cage. If you keep some smaller birds in the aviary, such as tiger finches (see page 118); which can also be let loose in the garden during the breeding process, then of course the shamas can be kept in such housing too. The aviary itself, however, should have sufficient hiding places in the form of thick shrubbery and undergrowth, because the hen leads a rather withdrawn life during the breeding cycle, since the male is constantly pursuing her. Once the young birds are ready to fly out, you will have to confine the cock (and the hen, too, of course), otherwise he will, along with his young, choose the freedom of nature instead of the aviary or cage.

These birds were first imported into Germany in 1880. They are very pleasant birds to keep and will reward the keeper with a great deal of enjoyment. Some of these birds have lived 15 years and longer in captivity, supplying enjoyment to their keepers with their charming movements and cheerful dispositions. This species should be brought indoors into a lightly heated area for the winter months.

Dyal Thrush (*Copsychus saulauris*): *Size*: 7 inches (18 cm). *Distribution*: Southern China, across to India, Sri Lanka, and Malaysia to Indonesia. *Clutch*: 4–5 blue-green eggs, marked with yellow, reddish-brown, or brown spots. *Incubation*: 11–12 days. *Fledging*: 12–13 days. Both hen and cock build the nest, but the hen hatches the eggs by herself, even though the cock brings her food regularly, even after the young have come out of the eggs. Apart from rearing food, you should also give them ant pupae, insects, and many mealworms. In addition, such things as stale soaked bread, cooked or finely cut raw ground beef, finely cut carrots, fruit, and hard-boiled egg white, should be served on a daily basis. The Dyal thrush makes an extremely timid cage bird but is a very pleasant aviary bird. If you allow them to pick a few mealworms out of your hand every day, they will soon become very tame and can be let loose outside like tame jackdaws. However, the hen should not be let loose during the breeding season, since you risk the

chance that the two birds will nest outdoors and after the breeding season is finished the family will take off. So allow only the male to fly loose, but have him back in the aviary by evening. I mention this only as general information, since I am personally not in favor of allowing these particular birds to fly loose. I feel it is better to keep them in an aviary well stocked with greenery. During the winter months these birds must be kept indoors in a lightly heated area. The birds love to bathe and often.

Tanagers

Tanagers (*Thraupidae*) are still considered to actually belong to the finch family (*Fringillidae*) by ornithologists. These small to medium-sized birds, however, will very seldom eat seeds or, in captivity, universal food; the majority of them have various types of fruits, berries, and even nectar as their main fare. They have short, rounded wings and are confined to the New World. The majority of these birds prefer to breed as high as possible in a variety of nesting boxes already containing nesting material in the form of coconut fibers, live and dead grass, leaves, moss, pieces of bark, wood, and the like.

Superb or Orange-rumped Tanager (*Tangara fastuosa*): *Size*: 5½ inches (14 cm). *Distribution*: Eastern Brazil. These tanagers spend their time high up in the crowns of trees, leaving only when they seek food. They breed together in small groups. *Clutch*: 2–4 pinkish-red eggs, almost fully marked with darker spots. *Incubation*: 13–14 days. *Fledging*: Approximately 14 days. In the aviary they like to hide and chase each other. They prefer to live in small groups, so in the aviary, if at all possible, try to keep a few pairs together. On warm, sunny days the birds will perch in the highest spots they can find in the greenery to enjoy the sun. Generally they are lively birds that become tame quickly and will even eat out of your hand.

The daily hosing off and the refreshing room-temperature bath water must not be forgotten. Apart from a large variety of fruit—berries; soaked, dried currants and raisins; grapes; cut pear and apple; dates; figs; bananas; and halved oranges—you should also offer a mixture of rusk crumbs, ant pupae, small mealworms, grated carrots, and finely chopped egg. Finely chopped red meat (without fat!) is also welcome. These beautiful birds can be kept in a roomy cage or aviary. If they are kept in a cage, the bottom needs to be covered daily, but never with sand! Offer shell grit in a separate dish. Since the birds consume a lot of fruit, their droppings will usually be thin.

Once the birds have become tame, it is perfectly all right to allow them to fly about inside the room where their cage is kept. It is best to allow this toward evening. The drapes need to be closed so that the birds do not injure themselves flying against the windows. In the meantime, you will be given a good opportunity to clean the cage and serve fresh food. When you want your bird to return to its cage, turn off the light in the room and turn on the one in the cage. These birds don't get along very well with other small birds in an outside aviary, especially in the breeding season; it occasionally happens that they steal the young birds out of the nests of the small exotic finches. Large birds can efficiently protect their nests, so it is fairly safe to keep this tanager species together with somewhat larger aviary birds.

Bread that has been soaked in milk and sprinkled with cane sugar or generously covered with natural honey is considered a real treat by these birds.

The speckled or yellow-browed tanager (*T. crysophrys* or *T. guttata*) from Costa Rica, Panama, eastern Colombia, Trinidad, Venezuela, and northern Brazil requires the same care and management.

Toucans

The often fairly strikingly marked toucans (*Ramphastidae*) are confined to the New World: the southern parts of Mexico, Central and South America to northern Argentina and southern Brazil. The very light, brightly colored bill has a spongy honeycomb interior structure, while the outer shell is extremely thin. In some cases the beak is almost as big as the rest of the body. All approximately 40 toucan species are arboreal birds, feeding on insects, fruits, and sometimes even fledging birds. They nest in tree holes and have 2–4 white eggs which are incubated by both sexes.

Cuvier's Toucan (*Ramphastos cuvieri*): *Size*: 18 inches (45 cm). *Distribution*: Northern South America. *Clutch*: 2–4 eggs. *Incubation*: 19–20 days. *Fledging*: 48–50 days. Toucans stand out because of their huge bills, which are built up out of hollow bone cells, which makes them very light, with only the edges hard and serrated. It is also strange that they completely lack the "beard" feathers around the beak. The birds have long tongues which are frayed at the edges. The area around the eye is unfeathered. Their wings are short and rounded, and the tail is also rounded. The birds walk very poorly because their first and fourth toes are directed backward. There are about 60 species in tropical America.

Their menu should be made up of fleshy fruits, berries, and insects. In their native land they probably also consume an occasional young bird or egg. Also give white bread, soaked rice, etc.

Toucans are very inquisitive but also calm birds. They like to have a high aviary, but do not behave well with fellow species or with small birds, particularly not at the feeding dishes!

In their native country toucans are hunted for their dark meat, which is considered tasty. They love to bathe, and frequently! They need thick perches for both sitting and sleeping; these should have a diameter of about 2½ inches (6½ cm).

The toco toucan (*R. toco*) from eastern South America—from the Guianas to northern Argentina—is also a very popular bird and requires similar care and management.

Training

First Steps Toward Successful Training

The first few days in a new home are stressful, but you must not give the new bird you wish to train too much rest. Start training immediately, and you'll have the best chances for success. As soon as the bird sits in its cage, carefully put your hand inside. For these initial overtures a strong, leather glove on your hand could be a wise precaution. The bird will soon accept your hand as being part of the "furniture" in the cage, especially if you move your hand slowly up and down. More than once, a young parrot has seated itself on my finger or hand within fifteen minutes of its arrival in my home.

As soon as the bird realizes that the hand inside does not change anything in the cage, nor harms it in any way, your new pet will accept your hand as a normal part of the cage. One bird will accept your hand sooner than another; in the latter case you will have to continue your efforts. Don't lose patience under any circumstance, because any unexpected movement of your hand will be experienced as something new. Move your hand slowly and wait until the bird accepts it. That should be your motto! As soon as the bird perceives that the hand put inside the cage is not a threat, it will examine it and after it has been approved, your hand will be accepted without much ado, as a "perch."

Once the bird is this far, put an index finger under the body very carefully, and press softly against the abdomen just above the legs; then the bird will usually obligingly seat itself on your outstretched finger. If this does not succeed at first, and the parrot, parakeet, or mynah flies away at the first few attempts, continue the first exercise, using the hand as the old familiar seat. If after a few days the hand is once more accepted without fear, try the finger method again.

Obviously, with large psittacines just an outstretched finger is not enough. Two or three fingers work better, or else use an outstretched hand. With small parrots and mynahs move the index finger softly but "coercively" across the abdomen; usually the bird will step over onto the finger. If the bird flutters wildly, under no circumstance must you withdraw your hand, as it may assume it has "scared away" your hand, and is therefore likely to repeat the action. Don't withdraw your hand from the cage before some success, however small it may be, has been achieved.

Outside the Cage

Once the bird sits on your finger (or hand), without any difficulties, it is wise to teach it also to step back from your finger (hand) to the perch. In order to accomplish this, hold the bird resting on your finger with its breast against a perch. An order, such as, "up," can be useful. When the bird fully knows this, take it out of the cage on your finger or hand. Prior to this several days may have passed. The first trip outside the cage must be of short duration. Of course the bird will probably at first fly around the room and inspect things. After a few days it will become evident that the bird chooses a special spot, usually close to a mirror, a window, or another shiny object in which it can see itself. Remember these places of preference, so you know where to look if the bird leaves the cage without your knowledge. Letting parrots fly around the room freely is quite risky, considering there may be fragile objects in the room. Also, most large parrots have a considerable wingspan and might easily injure themselves in the relatively small space of an average room.

A well-trained bird will return to the cage immediately if the trainer so wishes. At first, lure the bird back with some "goodies"; later on these "goodies" will not be needed. Again it is wise to use a fixed command, like "come!" If the bird refuses to "come," despite repeated requests, use a thin bamboo stick or a T-shaped perch. If you press the stick softly against the abdomen, the bird will usually climb onto it. Slowly move back to the cage, while your pet sits on the stick. But it is still important to train the bird so well, that it returns to the cage immediately after the command, "come!" If you have to go "bird-catching" all the time, not only will that be unpleasant and tiresome for the bird, but it will also be frustrating for you.

Once the bird will return directly to the cage whenever you wish, proceed to the next stage, which is teaching it to go from one hand to the other. Let it jump from one hand to the other as this is a very relaxing occupation for you as well as for the bird. When your pet understands that it may explore your arm or shoulder as well, you really have a "hand-tame" bird.

Training With a T-shaped Perch

A T-Shaped Perch most resembles a natural resting place and so is an excellent training tool. Many bird-trainers prefer using their finger during the first training sessions as mentioned above, others prefer a T-shaped perch. Such a perch must never be too smooth. If it is, it can be roughened up with sandpaper; of course, you should take care that there are no splinters on it.

But before going on, take note of this: perhaps you already know that birds cannot determine by appearance, whether they are dealing with male or female birds. Birds recognize gender through behavior; for example the generally greater aggressiveness of males when they look at each other. On the other hand, when a hen looks at a male, then the former will slant her head to one side or look away, and more or less ignore the male; or, if she is interested in the male, she will watch him closely while making nodding and bowing movements, her tail spread like a fan, and producing small clattering sounds with her beak. For this reason, it is a serious mistake to point a perch (or finger) straight at a sitting bird and slowly approach it. This resembles an approaching aggressive male.

The only way to approach a bird with a T-perch

To train your pet bird to perch on your finger, move the index finger against the abdomen just above the legs. Press softly and carefully. The bird will usually oblige by seating itself on the outstretched finger.

is from the side and very, very slowly indeed. As soon as the the parrot, parakeet, or mynah perceives the perch it is—if you play it right, that is—already very close by. You can now make the bird sit on the perch by pressing it softly against the abdomen (at the height of the feet). If the bird spots the perch sooner than you mean it to, move the perch slowly away from within its immediate reach and start anew by bringing the perch toward the bird from the side. It is not necessary to start all over from the other corner of the room; start right where you were standing when the bird perceived the T-perch. If it again backs away from the perch, wait until the bird has calmed down before making a new attempt. Again, stay right where you were with the last attempt.

The same procedure can be followed to get the bird out of the cage without using the hand-finger method, but with the help of a T-perch. Do not take the T-perch out of the cage until the parrot has learned to accept it as part of the cage furniture. Most cages have a detachable bottom, so the T-perch can be laid on the floor or placed against the bars. Sometimes it appears with this method that the bird reacts better and easier when approached from behind; the perch is moved across the back and head and under the abdomen in a semicircle and subsequently the bird is forced onto the perch by light upward pressure. Again, this upward pressure may be strong, so that if there is no reaction the bird is more or less slowly lifted from its seat. If the bird starts nodding nervously and appears to be getting jumpy, it is wise to wait until the bird has calmed down again, or else you risk having the parrot fluttering and scrambling about its cage restlessly. This will only make it more upset and perhaps afraid of the T-perch.

During the whole training period *talk* to your bird. It doesn't matter what you say, as long as you say something! The human voice often calms the bird and inspires trust in it. And don't give up the lesson unless the bird has made some progress, no matter how small it may be. In the case mentioned above, go on till the bird has placed itself on the T-perch, and after some well-meant, encouraging words, back to its usual perch. This is accomplished by pressing the T-perch against the abdomen, right next to the feet. This can sometimes be very tiresome for the trainer and it may take some time, but giving up is out of the question. The bird should learn *something* in a session, even if it is only a little, otherwise the rest of the training will become a difficult and tiresome occupation.

Clipping Wings

Clipping a few flight feathers to prevent the bird from escaping before it is completely tame is an aspect of our hobby on which I don't hold a definite opinion. I have worked with birds that have had their wings clipped as well as with birds that did not and I really couldn't say which birds were the easier

Clipping wings. Trim the secondary and all but the first 3–4 inner primary feathers on both wings. Never clip just one wing; the parrot would lose its balance when trying to take off, would tumble to the ground, and could seriously injure itself.

to work with. If you treat the bird in a calm, controlled manner it will not make a great difference, in my opinion; and of course it may also depend on the spirit of the various birds. I would therefore advise that you start training your birds without clipping their wings. If, however, your pupil proves rather obstinate, clipping a few flight-feathers can prove to be a very a good idea.

If you are for clipping, do it on both wings and with a sharp pair of scissors (see drawing above). Clipping a bird's wing won't hurt it, and after a while the clipped feathers will be replaced during molt by new ones. If the bird isn't fully trained when it starts growing new feathers, another clipping will be necessary.

Speech Training

Handle the mynah, parrot, or budgie calmly and try to gain its confidence. When you go to its cage say some words quietly, over and over again, for example, "Hello!" followed by its name. As soon as you are sure that the bird is not afraid of you, carefully open the cage door and slowly put your hand into the cage. If the bird panics, slowly remove your hand, close the door and wait until it settles down before trying again. A woman makes a better tutor than a man because she has a higher voice. A man, of course, can teach a bird to talk, but it is desirable that he try to pitch his voice a little higher. A bird trying to imitate a low-pitched voice is likely to talk hoarsely and not clearly.

• The first talking lesson consists of placing the bird on your finger and repeating one or two words over and over again in a loud and distinct voice. Do not say more than two words at first. It takes a young mynah generally two to three weeks to learn them; it usually takes young parrots and parakeets two to three months to learn the same words! If more words are said, the bird will be confused and will take a much longer time to learn them.

• Speak loudly because mynahs and all birds belonging to the parrot family like noise and pay more attention to a loud voice than to a soft, low one.

• Speak slowly. It is characteristic of the mynah, parrot, or parakeet, to speed up the words it is learning. If you speak fast, it will speak faster.

• Speak distinctly. Special emphasis should be given to each syllable.

• Lessons should be given as often as possible. The younger the bird and the more often it receives talking lessons, the sooner it will learn to talk. Shut out all other noises, hold the bird on your finger, and teach it systematically. Do this several times during the morning, several times during the afternoon and evening, and once when the bird is in the cage and covered up for the night. At other times of the day when you pass him in his cage or on his playground, repeat the words he is to learn. Do not say anything else but these words. Always use the same intonation. Different intonations of the same words will sound like different words to the bird; this may retard learning.

• When the bird repeats the initial words perfectly—the first word usually taught a bird is its name—it should be taught a short phrase. With systematic teaching, a mynah will have mastered such a phrase in a few days; it usually takes parrot-like birds about two weeks. If necessary, allow another week for the perfect mastery of the phrase; then proceed to teach the bird another short phrase.

• After the young bird has learned several phrases, a longer sentence may be taught. The more the bird learns, the quicker it will master new words. In teaching a sentence, always say the whole sentence through from beginning to end. If the bird does not repeat certain parts properly, do not correct those parts alone, but say the whole sentence again and again, emphasizing the syllables that have not been properly pronounced by the little pupil.

• There are some sounds a young bird does not like to repeat. *M, n,* and *l* are letters which should be used only sparingly when a baby bird is receiving his first talking lessons. Words starting with *p, t,* or *k* are quickly learned. Some young birds have difficulty pronouncing the letter *s* properly. Emphasis on words starting with an *s* will help to overcome this defect in diction.

• Mynahs and hookbills learn to repeat human language and other sounds best if they are tame, and attached to a person.

• One last, important, remark. It is not necessary to perform any kind of operation on a bird's tongue, as for instance cutting a tendon, to make it talk more clearly. This cruel practice is not justified in talking birds in general. The true vocal organ is the syrinx situated below the larynx and found in birds only. The tongue plays only a slight role in formulating all the minute differences in tone and accent which are so faithfully reproduced by these birds. For this reason, an injury to the tongue cannot lead to any improvement in talking and will do only harm!

Useful Literature and Addresses

Books and Magazines

Diemer, Petra. *Parrots*, Barron's, Hauppauge, New York, 1983.

Forshaw, Joseph M. *Parrots of the World*, 2nd edition, Lansdowne, Melbourne, Australia, 1981.

Frische, Dr. Otto von. *Canaries*, Barron's, Hauppauge, New York, 1983.

—*Mynahs*, Barron's, Hauppauge, New York, 1986.

Koepff, Christa. *The New Finch Handbook*, Barron's, Hauppauge, New York, 1984.

Lantermann, Werner. *The New Parrot Handbook*, Barron's Hauppauge, New York, 1987.

LaRosa, Don. *How to Build Everything You Need for Your Birds*, Audubon Publishing Company, Smithtown, New York, 1983.

Low, Rosemary. *The Complete Book of Parrots*, Barron's, Hauppauge, New York, 1989.

Martin, Hand-Jürgen. *Zebra Finches*, Barron's, Hauppauge, New York, 1985.

Moizer, S. and B. *The Complete Book of Budgerigars*, Barron's, Hauppauge, New York, 1988.

Sternigeweg, Werner. *The New Softbill Handbook*, Barron's, Hauppauge, New York, 1988.

Vriends, Matthew M. *Lovebirds*, Barron's, Hauppauge, New York, 1986.

—*Simon & Schuster's Guide to Pet Birds*, Simon & Schuster, New York, 1984.

Wolters, Annette. *African Gray Parrots*, Barron's, Hauppauge, New York, 1987.

—*Cockatiels*, Barron's, Hauppauge, New York, 1984.

—*Parakeets*, Barron's, Hauppauge, New York, 1983.

American Cage Bird Magazine
One Glamore Court
Smithtown, New York 11787

Bird Talk
P.O. Box 3940
San Clemente, California 92672

The AFA Watchbird
2208 "A" Artesia Boulevard
Redondo Beach, California 90278

North American Bird Clubs

American Federation of Aviculture
P.O. Box 1568
Redondo Beach, California 90278

American Cockatiel Society
1801 19th Avenue,
N.E. MPLS, Minnesota 55418

African Love Bird Society
P.O. Box 142
San Marcos, California 92069

Avicultural Society of America Inc.
8228 Sulphur Road
Ojai, California 93023

National Cockatiel Society
Rt. 1, Box 412
Equality, Alabama 36026

National Parrot Association
8 North Hoffman Lane
Hauppauge, New York 11788

Canadian Bird Clubs

Calgary and District Avicultural Society
7728 Bowcliffe Creek N.W.,
Calgary, Alberta T3B 2S5

British Columbia Avicultural Society
11784-90th Ave.
North Delta, British Columbia V4C 3H6

The Budgerigar and Foreign Bird Society
126 Grey-abbey Trail
West Hill, Ontario M1E 1V9

The Canadian Avicultural Society
32 Dronmore Cr
Willowdale, Ontario M2R 2H5

The Ontario Cage Bird Society
R.R. #5, Highway #24
Cambridge, Ontario N1R 5S6

Canadian Parrot Association
Pine Oaks R.R. #3
St. Catharines, Ontario L2R 6P9

Index

Numbers in *italic type* indicate color plates. *C1* indicates front cover; *C2*, inside front cover, etc.

Index

Index

Perfect for Pet Owners!